SLUM IMPROVEMENT THROUGH PARTICIPATORY URBAN-BASED COMMUNITY STRUCTURES

SLUM IMPROVEMENT THROUGH PARTICIPATORY URBAN-BASED COMMUNITY STRUCTURES

DR. S.L. GOEL
Emeritus Fellow, University Grants Commission
Formerly Member UGC, Member Distance Education Council
and Member All India Board of Management, AICTE
Professor of Public Administration (Retd.)
DCS, Panjab University, Chandigarh

and

DR. S.S. DHALIWAL
Additional Project Director,
State Urban Development Authority, Punjab,
Chandigarh

DEEP & DEEP PUBLICATIONS PVT. LTD.
F-159, Rajouri Garden, New Delhi-110027

SLUM IMPROVEMENT THROUGH PARTICIPATORY
URBAN-BASED COMMUNITY STRUCTURES

ISBN 81-7629-523-X

Typeset by ASHISH TECHNOGRAPHICS,
3190, Mohindra Park, Shakur Basti, Delhi-110034.

Printed in India at MAYUR ENTERPRISES,
WZ Plot No. 3, Gujjar Market, Tihar Village, New Delhi-110018.

Published by DEEP & DEEP PUBLICATIONS PVT. LTD.
F-159, Rajouri Garden, New Delhi-110027.
Phones: 25435369, 25440916
E-mail: ddpbooks@yahoo.co.in • deep98@del3.vsnl.net.in
Showroom:
2/13, Ansari Road, Daryaganj, New Delhi-110002 • Telefax: 23245122

Contents

Preface

Slums are dangerous both for slum dwellers as well as the population of the city where slums are located. How can we improve slums? Union, State and Local Governments have done a list of effort. Nothing substantial has been achieved.

Cities are engines of growth and slum dwellers are integral and essential participants in its development. Hence, they need to be included in the mainstream of the society by increasing their productivity and decreasing the inequality in society. The Slum Networking Project has shown that through the partnership concept, slums can be upgraded at a very low cost and slum dwellers find their own resources to upgrade their shelter, once infrastructure facilities and adequate tenure security is given. Provision of essential services alone is not enough, the softer interventions, through community development, which bring about attitudinal changes in the slum residents, are equally important.

The *"Cities Without Slums"* goal is now reflected as Target 11 of the Millennium Development Goals. Progress in achieving this goal will be monitored through two indicators: (i) the proportions of people with access to improved sanitation; and (ii) the proportion of people with access to secure tenure. The goal by 2020 is:

> "To have achieved a significant improvement in the lives of at least 100 million slum dwellers as proposed in the "Cities Without Slums" initiative."

Slums are a direct outcome of the failure of State policy and law to intervene effectively to ensure legal access of the urban poor to land and financial resources, which would be necessary to enable them to construct for themselves legal and adequate shelter. Despite stated commitment in official documents to ensuring access of housing to the poor, actual investments in this regard have been niggardly and misdirected. This is aggravated by both law as well as administrative and other prejudices which have not only consistently blocked the access of the urban poor to shelter but have actually criminalised them.

Slums are part of urban life; hence urban local bodies to eradicate it should spare no efforts. A good environment is key to development. Similarly, poverty is the mother of main problems. Its removal has gained importance world over in recent years. It cannot be tackled unless it is measured both qualitatively and quantitatively. I have examined large number of programmes aimed at poverty eradication especially the poverty of slum dwellers through participatory development of women.

However, a new philosophy, which believes in participation of slum dwellers, has shown some results. A study was undertaken in Punjabi to found out the advantages and problems of participation.

We are putting the facts, problems and suggestions for slum improvement. We are sure that the recommendations made here would be of great use for policy makers, planners and municipal staff to make the life of slum dwellers productive and useful.

Further, we would like to register our sincere gratitude to Sh. Bhim Singh and Ms. Neeru Bala for their untiring efforts in typing this manuscript. We also acknowledge the help of every individual for his or her efforts in bringing this book out. We are not in a position to acknowledge them individually but would like to register our sincere gratitude to all of them.

We are thankful to Sh. G.S. Bhatia of M/s Deep & Deep Publications Pvt. Ltd., New Delhi, who has brought this book out in a very short time.

Chandigarh

DR. S.L. GOEL
DR. 3S.S. DHALIWAL

1

Urbanization and Urban Development: Need of a Slum Policy

The urbanization process involves transformation of rural characteristics of people, their activities and their settlements to urban ones. It is the concentration of people engaged in non-agricultural land uses in human settlements that in turn provide the necessary economies of scale for the production and provision of specialized goods, infrastructure facilities and services. In the context of the development process, urban areas, depending on their size and type, spread innovations to their hinterlands through various forms of urban-rural and regional linkages. This diffusion process and the linkages give rise to different patterns of urban development, such as, development poles with distance decay patterns, corridor patterns, and rural-urban continuum.[1]

Urbanization is a world-wide phenomenon and urban population is growing at a faster rate than the average rate of growth of nation. It is a continuous process. Although India is not a highly urbanized country there has been a rapid growth of towns and cities during the last 40 years. Consequently, the urban population of the State of Punjab has also increased from 19.89 million in 1951 to 59.94 million in 1991.[2] (2001-Dr. Dhaliwal) and to 82.46 millions in 2001.

Before framing any national policy on urbanization and environmental problems, it will be absolutely necessary to bear the following facts in mind:

(i) Urbanization is a movement away from tradition in the direction of modernity.
(ii) Urbanization is shift of economy from agrarian to industrial.
(iii) Urbanization is a change of lifestyle from informal to formal.
(iv) Urbanization is a sign of material well-being, in terms of the physical comforts, which it promises to offer or actually offers.
(v) Urbanization is a change of sociological scale from the "little community" to the "mass society."
(vi) Urbanization is a change of human relations from deeply intimate and personal to highly segmental and impersonal.
(vii) Urbanization is a change of use of tolls of production from the manual to the mechanical.
(viii) Urbanization is a change of opportunities, including cultural interests, employment, etc. from the limited and somewhat boringly placid to almost infinite and thrillingly exotic.
(ix) Urbanization is a change of speed from the slow and steady pace of walking and horse/bullock-cart movement to 'fast and spurty' automobile locomotion.
(x) Urbanization is what thrives on the two principles of 'pull' (it attracts rural population by the allurement of facilities) and 'push (migration from out of the villages due to wide-spread poverty, unemployment and under-employment).[3]

A city literally means large town. In general usage the term 'city' is applied to any large and relatively dense concentration of population where the inhabitants are engaged primarily in non-agricultural occupations. Legal definitions are more specific. In the United States, a city is an incorporated municipality; the city's boundaries and powers of self-government are set forth in a charter from the State in which it is located.

A city has always symbolized the highest expression of human achievements. It is a depiction of architecture, a centre of art, learning, trade and commerce. It is here that the individualism takes birth and blossoms. It is here that vast multitudes congregate and become a microcosm of the nation, breaking traditional boundaries, combining smaller heterogeneous communities into a relatively homogenous people with new identities, Unfortunately, today cities have become very harsh places to live in.[4]

Most Third World nations are becoming increasingly urban. Cities of half a million, one million or several million people now dot the landscape, even in regions that were sparsely settled until a few decades ago. But Third World cities tend to grow physically and demographically without developing genuine resources to build indispensable infrastructure and services for their populations. The most Third World nations have not been able to raise their depressed-and depressing-levels of under-development. Cities, then, bear witness to the consequences of unequal global and national development, usually in the form of a multiplicity of degraded human environments.

The population of most large Third World agglomerations inhabits an area and utilizes space and services that were planned and built for a much smaller population. The result is a growing deficit in the basic equipment of all cities and a rapid rise in unemployment. Unskilled, unemployed or under-employed low-income households are particularly affected by this situation.

The poor of the cities are not true citizens of their own countries, for they have no political, social or economic rights. The poor age rapidly and they die young.

Poverty for urban poor means hunger, poor health, poor housing, inadequate social environments, illiteracy, lack of skills and very low incomes. But it also means living with little or no power to influence political life. In most Third World countries, a poor person is no more than a number in a census. Often, not even that official recognition is granted to them. They are not true citizens of their own countries for they have no political, social or economic rights.[5]

PROBLEMS AND CHALLENGES OF URBANIZATION

The then Hon'ble Minister for Urban Development, GOI, Sh. Jagmohan, had rightly spelled out the existing and emerging problems of Local-Self Government as follows:[6]

> "Invariably, cultural and civilization contours get imprinted on the faces of cities. The city has many facets. As an economic entity, it is a set of business and industry; as a social organization, it is a creator of community and collective action; as a political unit, it is a repository of old traditions, a fountain head of new ideas, an instrument of intellectual advancement, and a moulder of attitudes and thoughts. It is a spiritual workshop of the nation, a most imposing creation of its social, economic and cultural aspirations."

Urban policies, poverty, pollution, productivity, planning and pattern, and shortages (both physical and financial) are the crucial issues around which the machinery of urban governance in India revolves. The formidable nature of these issues has thrown this machinery in deep crisis. But this crisis is not merely of governance. It extends to the governed as well. It is a crisis of character, commitment, conscience, the creative and constructive sense of the community as a whole.

THE URBANIZATION SCENARIO IN INDIA

The Provisional Census Data of the 2001 Census reveals several significant facets of urbanization over the last decade. Of the 1.02 billion populations, 285 million or 27.8 per cent live in the urban areas, which comprise 5,161 towns, an increase of 2.1 per cent over the proportion of urban population in the 1991 Census. Table, 1.1 gives the proportion of urban population to total population between 1961 and 2001:

There is wide variation among states in urbanization. At one end of the spectrum is the National Capital Territory of Delhi, with 93 per cent of its population living in urban

TABLE 1.1

Proportion of Urban Population and Total Population

Year	*Per cent*
1961	17.97
1971	19.91
1981	23.34
1991	25.71
2001	27.78

Source: 10th Five-Year Plan, p. 612.

areas. At the other end, Himachal Pradesh is the least urbanized state with only 9.8 per cent of its population in urban areas. Tamil Nadu is the most urbanized among the larger states with 43.9 per cent urban population, followed by Maharashtra with 42.4 per cent and Gujarat with 37.4 per cent. Among the larger states, Bihar has the lowest proportion of urban population (10.5 per cent), below Assam (12.7 per cent) and Orissa (14.9 per cent).

In terms of absolute number of persons living in urban areas, Maharashtra leads with 41 million persons. Uttar Pradesh comes next with 35 million followed by Tamil Nadu with 27 million. (Annexure 1)

There are 27 cities with more than one million population, while the Urban Agglomerations (UAs)/Cities with population of more than one million number 35. About 37 per cent of the total urban population live in these Million Plus UAs/Cities. In Maharashtra, West Begnal and Gujarat, more than half of the urban population live in the Million Plus UAs/Cities.

The decadal growth of population in rural and urban areas during 1991-2001 is 17.9 per cent and 31.2 per cent respectively, indicating a relatively higher growth in urban population. However, it has been observed that the degree of urbanization in India is among the lowest in the world. United Nations estimates for 2000 show that 47 per cent of total population of the world lives in urban areas. While the proportion of urban population in developed countries range between 75 and 80 per cent, it is 36.7 per cent in Asia, Within Asia, countries like China and Indonesia, starting from lower levels of urbanization in 1950, have now overtaken India with urbanization of 32.1 per cent and 40.9 per cent respectively.

This is partly explained by one demographic fact: In India the decadal growth of urban population has been declining, from 46.1 per cent in 1971-81 to 36.4 per cent in 1981-91 to 31.2 per cent in 1991-2001. Correspondingly, the average annual exponential growth in UAs/Towns has also dropped from 3.8 per cent to 3.1 per cent and 2.7 per cent respectively. While this, to some extent, reflects a declining trend in total population growth, the fact still remains that urbanization in India is proceeding at a fairly modest pace, though some states and cities are reporting exponential growth.

The moderate growth rate gives some breathing space to set the house of urban governance in order. However, there are cities where there is no time to lose.[7]

The recent report of Census of India reveals that urbanization has increased to 31.13% between 1991 and 2001 as compared to 16% in 1951 and 29% in 1991. It is expected to touch the mark of more than 40% in 2021. Thirty-five cities in the country have crossed a population of over one million. Greater Mumbai with a population of 163.38 lacs, Kolkata with a population of 132.16 lacs and Delhi with 127.91 lacs, occupy first three positions respectively in 2001.The Punjab, which is known of its villages, has 33.95% of its population in the State is distributed over 157 towns out of which 14 towns have more than one lac population in 2001 as compared to 10 in 1991. The increase in urban population has created large number of problems for the Local-Self Government, which is already under great stress and strain. The problems faced by the urban local-self government do not merely limit themselves to traditional functions of providing basic services e.g. potable water supply, sewerage, waste disposal, etc. but extend to new and emerging problems of lawlessness, prostitution, rape, distress, thefts, crimes especially against women, unemployment, shelter, etc. thus, administration of cities has become complex, hence require the co-operation of all including adequate finance and especially the people's participation and involvement.

IMPACT OF URBAN GROWTH

Our cities are facing enormous problems and challenges. There is a growing concern about how to make our cities safe and sustainable. The cities which make vital contributions in the social and economic development are struggling with serious challenges such as environmental pollution, congestion, increasing incidence of urban poverty, inadequate access to shelter and basic services, increasing inequality in income levels resulting in the proliferation of slums and squatter settlements with overall deterioration in quality of life.[8]

Urbanization has created a number of problems, which would be discussed in other chapters. R.K. Arora and Rajini Goyal have rightly presented this complex situation.

The urban scene in India presents a series of paradoxes-growth and decay, poverty and affluence, slums and mansions, illiteracy and educational excellence, parochial groups and universalistic associations hope and despair, The urban centres are characterized by an inter-play of multi-level socio-political and economic forces, which cumulatively have added complexity to city life. This complexity poses enormous challenges to the administrative system involved in managing regulatory as well as developmental affairs in urban areas.

There is, in fact, evidence to show that urbanization is likely to have been a key determinant of economic growth in the 1980s and 1990s, boosted by economic liberalization. From this point of view, the moderate pace of urbanization in the country has been a cause of disappointment. There is, however, no rural vs urban conflict either in terms of national growth, or in development priorities. In fact, perhaps because of the success of rural development programmes along with the limited availability of land for squatting in central urban areas, there seems to be no runaway migration from rural to urban areas.

The impact of the growth of population on urban infrastructure and services has mostly been adverse. Cities with high rates of growth would be expected to have more resources for investment in the cities, but the fact is–that much of this potential has remained untapped. On the other hand, smaller cities with less economic growth face inadequacies of financial and other resources to cope with increasing demands on services, and this may call for supplemental support from the budget.

URBAN POVERTY

Poverty is the root-cause of all socio-economic problems. Poverty is a complex phenomenon. It manifests itself in a myriad ways. The poor not only suffer from low income and high unemployment, but also low life expectancy, low levels of literacy and poor health. Poverty is also perpetuated by vested sections of society.

In a broader sense the social dimensions of urban poverty have been adequately emphasized in the Report of the National Commission on Urbanization. It states:

> "poverty cannot be characterized adequately in terms of income, expenditure or consumption patterns alone... the focus should be on human degradation resulting from poverty. Thus, what is required is a multi-dimensional concept inclusive of the environment, access to services and social and psychological supports. The Commission believes that poverty has increased in the urban areas although some official figures don't show this."

The National Commission on Urbanization (1988) observed that Urban Poverty leads to:

(a) Proliferation of slums;
(b) Fast growth of informal sector;
(c) Increasing casualisation and under development of labour;
(d) Crushing pressure on Civic Services;
(e) High rates of Education deprivation and health contingencies; and

(f) Retarded growth of physical and mental capacities.

As poverty is one of the main reasons of deprivation, it is inevitable that women will be particularly vulnerable to needing or being required to become a point of attention. It has been seen that women struggle to reduce this vulnerability that poverty brings to their children.

10TH FIVE-YEAR PLAN OBSERVES

The encouraging feature is that apart from continuation of the fall in the proportion of the urban poor, for the first time in the 1991 Census, there is also a reduction in the absolute numbers of the urban poor. According to the large sample survey data on consumer expenditure (55th Round) of the NSSO using a 30 day recall period, 67.1 million or 23.62 percent of India's urban population were below the poverty line in 1999-2000. As is evident from the Table 1.2, while the percentage of persons below poverty line in urban areas had been steadily declining since it was first estimated at 49 per cent in 1973-74, the absolute number of persons below the poverty line had been rising, touching 76.3 million in 1993-94. This trend has been reversed in the latest Census.

Though, at the national level, the percentage of the poor in rural areas is significantly higher than in urban areas, only a few of the larger States conform to this pattern. States such as Andhra Pradesh, Goa, Gujarat, Haryana, Karnataka, Kerala, Madhya Pradesh, Maharashtra, Rajasthan, Tamil Nadu, Delhi and the Union Territory of Pondicherry have reported levels of urban poverty that are higher than rural poverty. States where rural poverty is higher than in urban area are Arunachal Pradesh, Assam, Bihar, Himachal Pradesh, Orissa, Uttar Pradesh and West Bengal. Analysis shows that poverty reduction among States has been uneven. The most important point about the inter-state variations in poverty is that it shows no correlation with per capita income or other development indicators like per capita consumption, levels of industrial and infrastructural development, etc., in urban areas during the nineties. While the lack of development is the cause of urban poverty in may States, the nature and sectoral composition of development is responsible for poverty in others.

Unemployment data show that the overall unemployment rates are not high, though they are higher in urban areas than in rural areas. The unemployed person-day rates are higher than the rates obtained for persons, thereby indicating a high degree of intermittent unemployment. This is mainly due to the absence of regular employment for many workers. Studies have shown that casualization of labour is the main, and increasing source of urban poverty. The dynamics of development in urban areas of many States during the past two decades has been such that rapid economic growth has not led to a corresponding decline in poverty. While income levels are rising to meet the basic nutritional needs, other equally basic needs of shelter, civic amenities, health care, educational and social needs, etc. are not being met in an adequate fashion. Urban poverty, thus, emerges as a more complex phenomenon than rural poverty.

Level of Basic Amenities

There are serious deficiencies in urban infrastructure as a result of the rapid growth of urban population and low investment in urban development. In general, the smaller the town, the less likely it is to have a wide coverage of amenities, and the poor in such towns face correspondingly higher deprivation. It has been noted that the percentage of households having flush toilets exhibits a strong positive correlation with economic development, much more than any other indicator of amenities. The coverage of civic amenities, specifically electricity, drinking water and toilets, is uneven and variation across size class of urban centres shows regularity and a distinct pattern. The percentage of households covered by each of the three amenities increases systematically with the size class of the urban centres except for Class VI towns. Class V towns (population between 5,000 and 10,000) register a high percentage of households not covered by toilets, electricity and drinking water (61 per cent, 41 per cent, and 28 per cent respectively) in 1991. The shortages are very serious for urban centres with population of less than 50,000. This emphasizes the need for greater involvement of the State and Central Governments in upgrading the infrastructure of the small towns. Most of the small and medium towns are not in a position to generate funds to provide civic amenities to all sections of population. These towns, particularly those located in less developed states, should, therefore, be the major focus of government policy in terms of providing basic amenities.

MAJOR ISSUES IN URBANIZATION

Attitudes to urban growth within the country tend to swing between two extremes. Cities are seen either as an unavoidable evil or in a more positive way as 'engines of growth'. Those who focus on the growth of slums and squatter colonies, the congestion on the roads and environmental degradation, hold the former view. The others, in contrast, focus on the bustling formal and informal sectors in urban areas and their contribution to the economy, the diversification of occupations away from traditional land-based ones to newer forms of production and services, and the lower levels of poverty as compared to rural areas.

TYPES OF VULNERABILITY OF THE POOR

Housing Vulnerability

Lack of tenure, poor quality shelter without ownerships rights, no access to individual water connection/toilets, unhealthy and in-sanitary living conditions.

Economic Vulnerability

Irregular/casual employment, low paid work, lack of access to credit on reasonable terms, lack of access to formal safety net programmes, low ownership of productive assets, poor net worth, legal constraints to self-employment.

Social Vulnerability

Low education, lack of skills, low social capital/caste status, and inadequate access to food security programmes, lack of access to health services, exclusion from local institutions.

Personal Vulnerability

Prone to violence or intimidation, especially women, children, the elderly, disabled and destitute, belonging to low castes and minority groups, lack of information, lack of access to justice.

APPROACH TO URBAN POVERTY ALLEVIATION

In an environment, where the poor are exploited and ignored, there is a major role for the State and its agencies, including the ULBs and the parastatals, in the field of urban development and provision of services such as water supply, health, education, sanitation, legal protection and employment generation. This is an immense challenge because of the known weaknesses of the system like the lack of accountability, corruption, and the dominant role of elite groups who wield substantial power in urban governance.

The first formal attempt to experiment with the community development approach in cities was the Urban Community Development project started in 1958. The Environmental Improvement of Urban Slums scheme was started in 1972 at the Central level to provide basic physical facilities like safe drinking water, sanitation, storm water drains, street lighting and roads. This scheme was transferred to State Governments in 1974. Following experiments with a variety of combinations of schemes for employment generation, formation of beneficiary groups, training, community organizations and thrift/self-help groups, finally the integrated programme of Swarn Jayanti Shahri Rozgar Yojana (SJSRY) was launched in 1997.

The implementation of programmes for the urban poor is beset with enormous problems. The problem of inadequate funding has been compounded by under-utilization of Central funds, diversion of funds released for specific programmes, and infructuous expenditure. Monitoring at the Central level has been weak and ineffective. Success stories have not been publicized or adopted on a wider scale. The understanding of the programmes, their objective and modalities relating to

TABLE 1.2

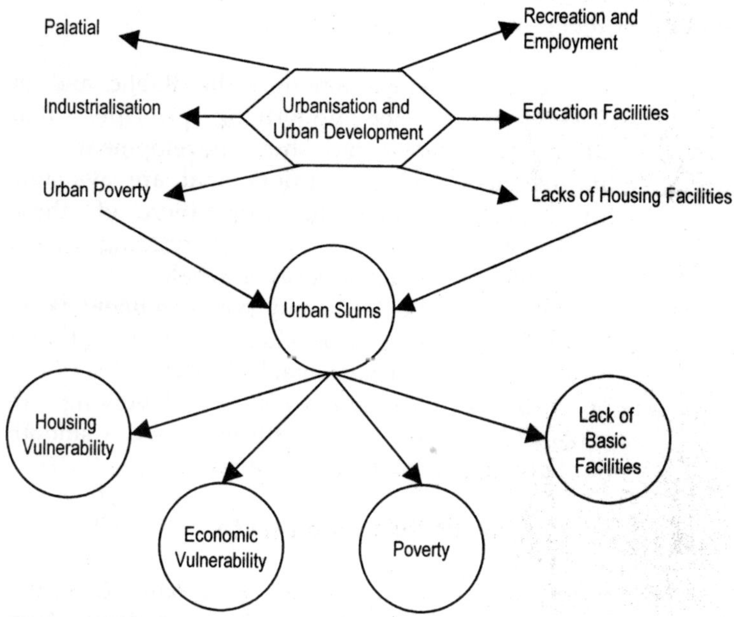

implementation has been weak and superficial, leading to inaction in many areas that are of vital concern to the urban poor. There are few master plans and very little effort at monitoring the benefits that are expected to flow to the target communities. In addition, there has been too much emphasis on engineering or the 'works' aspects of programmes without adequate understanding of the social, psychological and other dynamics of poverty. The beneficiaries have not been consulted nor given a voice in the implementation of programmes. When there is a deceleration of economic growth, especially when governments experience fiscal constraints and need to reduce deficits, allocation of funds for the social sectors suffers. This should not happen.[9]

To overcome the negative impact of urban development i.e. creation of slums, there is need of National Slum Policy, which can act as a guideline to action i.e. slum improvement. The Government of India has come out with a draft National Slum Policy (Draft), April 1999, which need to be made into an Act and implemented Toquote:

The main objectives of Governing Principles and Essential Strategic Interventions:

1. To create awareness amongst the Public and in Government of the underlying principles that guide the process of slum development and improvement and the options that are available for bringing about the integration of these settlements and the communities residing within them into the urban area as a whole.
2. To strengthen the legal and policy framework to facilitate the process of slum development and improvement on a sustainable basis.
3. To establish a framework for involving all stakeholders for the efficient and smooth implementation of Policy objectives.

GOVERNING PRINCIPLES

1. Slums are an integral part of urban areas and contribute significantly to their economy both through their labour market contributions and informal production activities. This Policy, therefore, endorses an upgrading and improvement approach in all slums. It does not advocate the concept of slum clearance except under strict guidelines set down for resettlement and rehabilitation in respect of certain slums located on untenable sites.
2. The Policy embodies the core principle that households in all urban informal settlements should have access to certain basic minimum services irrespective of land tenure or occupancy status.
3. Cities without slums should be the goal and objective of all urban planning for social and economic development. To reach this goal, it will be necessary to re-vision our urban development processes to make towns and cities fully

democratic, economically productive, socially just, environmentally sustainable, and culturally vibrant.

4. Urban growth and development should lay greater emphasis on equity and distributive justice. This will mean adopting policies and processes that promote balanced, equitable and sustainable development. The policy aims to support the planned growth of urban areas in a manner that will help to upgrade all existing slums and informal settlements with due regard for the protection of the wider public interest.
5. The proliferation of slums and informal settlements can be obviated by ensuring continuous supply/recycling of serviced and semi-serviced land suitable for high-density occupation by lower income groups. Institutional planning and fiscal mechanisms should be devised to prevent the idle use of land in urban areas. In those few cases where land needs to be conserved for future use in the wider public interest, the land owning agencies concerned must evolve more effective safeguarding measures.
6. Urban local bodies should work in collaboration with all other stakeholders to enhance the impact of slum development and improvement activity by building the capacities of the poor and empowering them to improve their own living conditions. Urban management systems need to be improved in three critical areas: (i) resource allocation and use; (ii) service delivery; and (iii) urban governance—democratic, efficient, transparent and gender sensitive.
7. The poor represent an extremely important element of the urban labour force and contribute substantially to total productivity and labour market competitiveness. It is vital that all ULBs recognize the contribution of the urban poor in helping to build urban prosperity and make sufficient provision for them to have access to affordable land, house sites and services. The

present planning and development framework is exclusive of slums and informal settlements. It views slums as "problem areas" requiring corrective action. The legal framework with its origin in the pre-independence socio-economic context requires modifications and progressive change. There is a need for a greater commitment to institutional re-orientation by adopting a more 'enabling' approach to the delivery of basic services accessible to the poor through the more effective mobilization of community resources and skills to complement public resource allocations. Major areas of attention include: town planning, land management, poverty alleviation, basic service delivery and capacity building.

8. Greater participation of communities and civil society in all areas of planning, capacity building and development is envisaged. The 74th Constitution Amendment represents the context within which this Policy document is set, recognizing that it is the ultimate responsibility of States and urban local bodies to interpret and implement this policy to the best of their ability. This policy reinforces the emphasis in the 74th Constitutional Amendment on decentralized participatory structures such as ward Committees and Municipal Planning Committees in support of local initiatives by community groups. This policy stresses, inter-alia, a priority role for local bodies in the discharge of functions listed in the Twelfth Schedule viz: (i) slum improvement and upgradation; (ii) urban poverty alleviation, (iii) regulation of land use and construction of buildings, (iv) provision of urban amenities, and (v) public health and sanitation including provision of water supply.
9. In line with the 74th Amendment this Policy presumes that all public land not identified for specific government use should be vested with the ULB.

ESSENTIAL STRATEGIC INTERVENTIONS

1. "Inclusive" Approach to Definition of Slum/Informal Settlement

(a) All under-serviced settlements, be they unauthorized occupation of land, congested inner-city built up areas, fringe area unauthorized developments, villages within urban areas and in the periphery, irrespective of tenure or ownership or land use shall be covered under the definition of a slum/informal settlement.

(b) The criteria for defining a slum/informal settlement shall take into consideration economic and social parameters (including health indicators) as well as physical conditions. Each State/Union Territory shall lay down the norms/criteria for categorizing an area as under-serviced and the local body of each town shall list all such areas as slums.

2. Listing and Registration

(a) Comprehensive Listing of Slums/Informal Settlements

For the purpose of providing basic urban services, all under-serviced settlements characterized by poor physical and socio-economic conditions irrespective and land tenure status and ownership should be identified and demarcated from regular planned neighbourhoods inhabited by better off residents. Once identified, the urban local body should list these settlements.

(b) Registration of Slum Dwellers

All people residing in such listed settlements should then be registered with the ULB in order to prevent ineligible beneficiaries being included in development programmes and schemes just before the initiation of improvement works or the issue of tenurial rights. The date for the completion of this process will be at the discretion of the ULB. A reckoning date will be required for administrative purposes in order to facilitate annual planning, budgeting and service provision. The register should be updated to include subsequent amendments and new registrations lodged with Ward Committees from time to time.

(c) Identity Card

A suitable identity card shall be issued to all households in listed slums. The identity card may contain a few details such as household name, address, details of family members etc.

(d) Basic Service Eligibility

Once settlement have been listed in the above manner all registered residents will be automatically eligible to receive basic minimum services/amenities from the urban local bodies (ULB), pending any more permanent measures taken to upgrade, rehabilitate or resettle the community. Each State and ULB should determine the norms and standards for basic services such as water, sanitation, electricity, health, etc. and how these will be delivered to residents of listed settlements.

(e) Other Entitlements

All urban poor, regardless of their land tenure status, shall be entitled to any other special assistance or welfare schemes that are operative within the urban area and/or the State and which are not geographically or spatially determined but targeted to specific poverty groups. These may include schemes for economic support, credit, pensions, insurance etc and services.

3. De-listing

The urban local bodies should de-list those settlements, which have been provided with a sustainable level of basic services, and where socio-economic indicators have reached defined acceptable norms. ULBs may also consider prescribing a certain period of time (two or three years) for providing basic services under any slum development programmes after which the area should be reviewed for de-listing.

4. Classification of Land Status/Tenability

The land status of all listed slums/informal settlements should be classified by the ULB as either Tenable or Untenable in order to determine whether or not regular planned service provision will be undertaken on an in-situ or re-settlement basis. All listed slums/informal settlements should be considered as Tenable unless the site falls strictly within the definition of Untenability as expressed below:

(a) Definition of Untenable Slums/Informal Settlement

A site shall not be declared as untenable unless existence of human habitation on such sites entails undue risk to the safety or health or life of the residents themselves or where habitation on such sites is considered contrary to "Public Interest".

The issue of whether a settlement's existence is against public interest shall be decided by the District Magistrate in consultation with the ULB and technical experts, after giving full opportunity to the resident community to express their views, in a public hearing. The process of consultation and public hearing shall be completed within three calendar months from the date of their initiation.

(b) Definition of Tenable Slums/Informal Settlements

All listed settlements that do not fall strictly within the category identified above under untenable situations shall be considered 'Tenable', and thus eligible for in-situ upgrading (subject to the settlement of ownership disputes on private land).

5. Granting of Tenure

(a) Tenure on Government Owned Land

Tenure shall be granted to all residents on tenable sites owned or acquired by government. Full property rights shall be granted on resettlement and/or rehabilitation sites. Tenure shall be allotted in the joint names of the head of household and spouse, subject to the proviso that single women or single men headed households shall not be precluded from having full tenure rights. Other forms of tenure may also be considered, if desired by the community. This may include: group tenure, collective tenure, co-operative tenure etc.

Conflict Resolution

On lands occupied by Slums/Informal Settlements and owned by Central, State and Local Government bodies, Municipal Authorities are to be designated as nodal agencies for initiating the process of resolution of disputes. It will be obligatory for Ministries at the state and central level to participate in these negotiations. The Ministry of Urban Affairs and Employment M (UAE) will play a pro-active role in resolving disputes on such lands owned by Union Ministries so that all basic services, development and resettlement and rehabilitation (R&R) activities can be negotiated more effectively. The M (UAE) may be empowered to act as an arbitrator between Central Government and local bodies concerning disputes over such lands (owned by Union Government).

(b) Tenure on Privately owned lands

(i) Land Acquisition

All Tenable settlements on private land should be acquired unless the ULB decides to pass a resolution otherwise. All states should make immediate provision to streamline and simplify the procedure to ensure the speedy acquisition of land for slums on private land categorized as Tenable. The land acquisition process should be completed within a maximum period of six calendar months from the time of initiating the process.

(ii) Negotiated Compensation

The acquisition of land from private parties should be undertaken on a negotiated basis. All the stakeholders (residents, urban local bodies, public agencies, others) may be invited to participate in the negotiation to promote transparency and equity. Funds earmarked from a tax/cess on vacant lands should be drawn from the Urban Poverty Eradication and Shelter Fund to provide compensation for acquiring private lands on which the slum settlements exist. Compensation may include monetary contributions, sharing of land, lease of land, allocation of an alternate site etc.

(c) Residents Association

At the time of granting tenure, it should become a prerequisite for the residents to form an association/society, which must be recognized by the urban local body. This association/society should normally consist of all resident families in that area, where one woman represents each family.

(d) Land Use Classification

Land use for in-situ up gradation projects should be designated as high density mixed use. This will be subject to the condition that any commercial/industrial/trading ventures permitted on such lands shall only be those, which are non-polluting; environment friendly and which provide employment to local slum dwellers.

(e) Layout Planning

In the in-situ upgrading projects, proper layout planning including plot re-alignment and also preferably equalization of land/shared land areas should precede the granting of full property/tenure rights. This should be under taken on a participatory basis with local residents.

(f) Sale of Tenure/Property Rights

A fee should be collected from residents for the sale or transfer of ownership rights based on the following criteria:

- A plot area up to a maximum of 25 sq. mts. may be granted at a concessional rate;
- Any area in excess of this may be granted at such rates decided by the ULB;
- Plot sizes may be fixed below 25 sq. mts. if mutually agreed by the community and the ULB.

(g) Sale of House Plots

While this policy would like to ensure that, as far as possible, house plots remain with the original allottees, it also recognizes that any over regulation of the property market will simply lead to the flourishing of a "black market". With a view to obviate this, the policy would not wish to prevent any poor household from realizing the value of their asset should they be forced to sell for any legitimate reason (such as loss of income, death, etc.) provided that any sale of plot/ title meets with the approval of the residents association/ULB established under (c) above and where the property is preferably sold back to the same association/ULB. The association/ULB should consider levying a tax/charge on all such sales to ensure that a proportion of any increase in land value realized from such a sale or transfer is utilized for communal benefit. The levying of taxes or charges by a Resident Association or similar organization will require special legal or administrative actions.

6. Resettlement and Rehabilitation

It is to be emphasized in keeping with the principles of this Policy, that this document primarily endorses and promotes an upgrading and improvement approach to deal with slums and informal settlements as opposed to resettlement. However, where habitation is on a site categorized as Untenable as indicated under Section 4 above, the following guiding principles are enumerated to safeguard the interest of residents in such settlements:

Those residing in listed settlements classified as Untenable are entitled to receive basic minimum services until proper relocation and resettlement provisions have been established and met. All States/ULBs must draw up comprehensive resettlement and relocation guidelines for urban dwellers and all relocation or resettlement of dwellers residing in untenable sites shall be implemented strictly in accordance with such guidelines, which should ensure that:

(a) Alternatives to resettlement should be fully explored before any decision is taken to move people.

(b) Relocation distances should be minimized to reduce the impact on livelihoods.
(c) Resident dwellers must be provided with some choice of alternative sites and where feasible, an alternative rehabilitation package.
(d) All resettlement sites should be adequately serviced and provision should be made for public transportation prior to settlement.
(e) The livelihoods of affected people must be sufficiently compensated within a fixed period.
(f) Participation of primary stakeholders, particularly women, in planning and decision-making is a pre-requisite for any resettlement process.
(g) Women's particular needs and constraints must be specifically addressed.
(h) Any urban development project that leads to the involuntary resettlement of communities must make provision to cover the costs of R & R.
(i) All stages of the resettlement process including the transition and follow-up period should be closely monitored and supervised by the ULB with community representatives. (Also see section 16 on monitoring and evaluation)

Translating these principles into action envisages:

- Full, accurate and detailed baseline inventories of all assets including livelihoods;
- Community mobilization;
- Timing of the interventions to reduce dislocation and discomfort especially during periods of inclement weather;
- Communication at all levels to ensure transparency;
- Mobilizing support of the local media to assist the process;
- Co-ordination of multiple ministries and convergence of various programmes;
- Participation of the host community at all states of the process;

- Granting land tenure rights;
- Monitoring and evaluating.

In addition the policy suggests the following:

Strengthening Municipal Governance and Management

(a) Urban Governance

The nature of urban governance has important implications for national slum development policy, which requires the adoption of new approaches to urban management and urban poverty alleviation. Urban governance should be defined as the relationship between civil society and the municipality/ULB. This implies a shift away from a perspective that defines infrastructure and services provision as exclusive concerns of government, to all new perspective that acknowledges the potential role, responsibility and impact of civil society. Civil society groups include: civic associations, community groups, women's groups, social movements, non-governmental organizations, community-based organizations, private sector etc. etc. These groups already play a significant role in areas such as housing development, sale and rental of land, transportation and enterprise.

The 74th Constitutional Amendment Act shall form the basis for converging new partnerships and creating an environment where in the urban local body as the city government will have the prime responsibility as a coordinator. One of the important features of the 74th Amendment is the constitution of Ward Committees, which should be extended to cover local bodies of all sizes. In particular community structures of the poor should nominate Ward Committee members rather plan than political parties.

In keeping with the spirit of the 74th Constitutional Amendment, the activities, which are hitherto performed by state level agencies like slum clearance board, Housing Board etc., needs to be operated through the local body. Till such time the institutional restructuring is not fully accomplished, the local body in each town shall mandatorily be consulted and shall guide all activities of such state level agencies particularly with regard to provision of amenities and services.

(c) Capacity Building

A series of capacity building initiative should be promoted to enable ULBs to effectively carry out slum development in accordance with National Slum Development Policy. This should include skill development, financial administration and management and human resource development.

(i) Skill Development

Skill Development shall be taken up under a three-tier training strategy covering:

- Seminars for senior level functionaries (both officials and elected representatives);
- Mid carrier training at decentralized locations;
- On-the-job training.

Skill Areas

- Listing of slums and identification of eligible households;
- Classification of Slums;
- Assessment of overall requirements for slum development in the town and preparation of IMDP;
- Mobilization of Slum Community in a three tire structure in line with CDS;
- Preparation of Annual Action/Investment plans;
- Development of projects for in-situ development and resettlement of slums;
- Identification of modes and modalities to involve Private Sector, NGOs etc. in the implementation on IMDP.

(ii) Financial Management

This component will be essential to the implementation

of improved financing of slum development. It will be necessary to build financial management capacity in a number of areas such as:

- Asset Management—development of inventory, classification, valuation, assessment of returns and mobilization strategy;
- Financial Planning—normative budgeting and investment Planning;
- Accounting and internal control—application of double entry accounting, reporting and recording formats and timely auditing.
- Borrowing and Debt Management—updating of debt register and optimum recovery from assets created by debt;
- Automation—asset, receivable, payable accounting, budgeting;
- Property Tax Reforms;
- Public Private Partnerships.

(iii) Human Resource Development

Human resource management and development shall cover the promotion of specific cadre under community development cell within ULB to prepare, implement and monitor IMDP at town level. The deployment of cadre at ULB level shall be for a minimum prescribed period so as to have continuity in the slum development activity.

(iv) Multi-lateral and bi-lateral Cooperation should be promoted to have Financial and Technical Support to carry out capacity building and develop a backup of research, evaluation and impact assessment studies for dissemination in a wider context of skill development. This should be taken up by direct contribution to slum development funds as well as implementation of demonstration projects.

(d) Partnership

In order to realize the above-suggested changes, it will be necessary to consider practical ways of developing partnerships with civil society groups for the improvement of informal settlements. Partnerships need to be institutionalized and not person based. For achieving this, there is a need to create a mandate for partnerships and recognize capacity building as a thrust area in programmes with definite budgets and plans. Capacity building should be applicable across the board to communities, officials, NGOs, non-officials (elected representatives) and all stakeholders.

Partnership Principles: Important guiding principles for partnership development shall include:

(i) Widening the base to include a wide variety of community organizations like youth groups, Mahila Mandal, saving and credit groups, association of interest groups/trades etc., and give thc interlinking responsibility to the community development unit;

(ii) The nature of financial inter-mediation should be such that, it facilitates creation of community based financial institutions suitable to local needs and situations;

(iii) Women should share decision-making with the local body, so as to learn to do the same on their own when they become more active as memebrs or managers in local CBOs;

(iv) Invest in capacity building in respect of various activities and ensure dovetailing of training with the activity itself; for instance balwadi teachers may require skill training and encouragement for the innovative use of using local material and models in the day-to-day teaching activity;

(v) CBOs must have a choice to select from a range of technical or professional expertise in legal, infrastructure, sanitation, and other aspects with local body assistance;

(vi) Develop flexible instruments to facilitate infrastructure development to be demanding driven and evolving.

(d) Community Development

To give a focus and direction for establishing partnership arrangements, in particular between the communities and the departments of the local body, a nucleus of community development unit has to be established in each and every local body. This unit should take a lead role in converging all activities of slum development through community organizations, NGOs and other civil society actors.[10]

CONCLUSION

Slums have become a necessary evil. The slums are not the places, which cannot be removed. There is a need of slum policy, which can take care of slum dwellers and make them a decent partner of urban life. This requires a political will and courage among the persons living in slums.

Notes and References

1. Tiwari, V.K., 'National Seminar on Future Cities—Urban Vision: 2001', p. 3.
2. Dhaliwal, S.S., 'Municipal Administration', Deep and Deep Publications, New Delhi, p. 1.
3. Bhatti, S.S., "Challenges of Urbanization and Environmental Problems in Revamping Urban Governments in India,' Ed. By Pradeep Sachdeva, New Delhi, Kitab Mahal, pp. 16-17.
4. Khurana, M.L., 'Cities for All', Shelter, Vol. II, Nos. 3 and 4, July-October, 1999, pp. 30-31.
5. Jorge E. Hardoy, 'World Health', The magazine of the World Health Organization, International Year of Peace, July 1986, pp. 12-13.
6. 'City Lights', Hindustan Times, December 14, 2000.
7. Government of India, Planning Commission, Tenth Five-Year Plan (2002-2007), (Draft), Volume II, Sectoral Policies and Programmes, pp. 612-613.
8. Jenia, P.K., 'Challenges of 21st Century Cities in Indian Agenda for Action', Shelter, Vol. II, Nos. 3-4, July-Oct., 1999. p. 64.
9. Government of India, Planning Commission, Tenth Five Year Plan (2002-2007), Volume II, Sectoral Policies and Programmes, p. 627.
10. GOI: Ministry of Urban Affairs and Employment, National Slum Policy (Draft), New Delhi, April 1999, pp. 1-9 & 28-31.

2

Urban Slums: Issues and Problems

SLUMS

Slums are cancerous for urban life and no effort should be spared to eradicate them. No doubt, they are manifestation of socio-economic conditions prevailing in the country, but if no heed is paid to contain them, urban life will become not only miserable but also unbearable. A serious policy of urban development, based on sound principles of town planning and efficient administration, committed to the service of the humanity with vast financial resources and authority can only successfully combat the problems of slums.[1]

Slums are a bye-product of urbanization and industrialization. Slum-dwellers are the real architect of urban facilities but their own life is endangered with poor facilities made available to them. Because of the laxity on the part of the municipal government, these slums sprang up and later on become difficult to control.

GENESIS OF SLUMS AND MAGNITUDE OF THE PROBLEM

"Slum" is defined as that area where the buildings are in any respect unfit for human habitation; or by reason of dilapidation, overcrowding, faulty arrangement of buildings, streets, lack of ventilation, light or sanitation facilities or combination of these factors, are detrimental to safety, health or morals (Slums Improvement and Clearance Act, 1956). Approximately, 68.8% of the country's slums population is concentrated in the 300 Class I cities and less than 1/3rd of this population resides in the remaining 3300 urban centers.[2]

Slums are not fit for settlement and are a danger both for residents and the urban population living nearby. Roosevelt has rightly said that poverty anywhere is a danger to prosperity.

Sh. Aditya Prakash, retired Principal of the College of Architecture, Chandigarh, has termed the growth of slums in the City Beautiful of Chandigarh, as a "planning failure". He says:

> "The slums should not have been allowed to sprout in the first place. The need of the hour is to solve poverty and shelter problems and it can be done through proper planning".

EVOLUTION OF SLUMS

Urbanization has been considered as an index of development but in case of developing countries like India, urbanization is not the outcome of merely the growth potential generated by urban settlements. It has been largely due to people work relationship in rural areas, in which land is the essential medium and which is right now so critically balanced that even small addition to population is pushing people out of agriculture to non-agricultural occupations. Thus, by and large, in India urbanization is merging as merely a process of transfer of rural poverty to urban environment, which only results in concentration of misery. This has resulted in the malfunctioning of most of the urban settlements leading to emergence of number of imbalances and problems. Thus, most of these settlements suffer from improper and haphazard development, absence of basic infrastructure and services, uncontrolled and unchecked growth of slums, lack of housing, high degree of visual and environmental degradation and uncontrolled traffic. The cumulative effect of these factors is the degradation of quality of life in urban settlements and huge amount of subsidies is required to maintain them. These facts are more evident in case of larger cities especially metros and super metros.

PROBLEMS OF URBAN AREAS ESPECIALLY HUMAN SETTLEMENTS

Urban areas have not received much attention in terms of the planning, development and management despite the fact that cities and economic development are inextricably linked. Because of high productivity of urban areas, economic development activities get located in cities. Accordingly, it is desirable that human settlements are provided with necessary planning and development inputs so that the orderly growth and development is ensured. This would also be necessary for ensuring efficient functioning of human settlements for improving their productivity and for providing desirable quality of life to its residents in order to cater to their both economic and physical and metaphysical needs. The urban development strategy for any state thus assumes importance of not only its economic emancipation but also its physical well being.

CONCEPT OF SLUMS[3]

The concept of slums and its definition vary from country to country depending upon the socio-economic conditions of each society. Irrespective of location, whether in the core of the city, in the form of old dilapidated structures or in the outskirts, in the form of squatting, Slums have often been characterized.

(a) Physically, an area of the city with inadequate housing, deficient facilities, overcrowding and congestion.

(b) Socially, slum is a way of life, a special character which has its own set of norms and values reflected in poor sanitation, health values, health practices, deviant behaviour and social isolation.

(c) Legally speaking, section 3 of the Slums Areas

(Improvement and Clearance) Act, 1956 defines slums as areas where buildings:

(i) are in any respect unfit for human habitation; and

(ii) are by reason of dilapidation, over-crowing, faulty arrangements of streets, lack of ventilation, light or sanitation facilities or any combination of these factors which are detrimental to safety, health and morals.

The slum areas are declared by a notification in the official gazette, which require:

(a) repair,
(b) stability,
(c) natural light and air,
(d) system of dump,
(e) water supply,
(f) drainage and sanitary conveniences, and
(g) facilities for storage, preparation of cooking of food and disposal of waste water, the buildings deemed to be unfit if it is so ineffective in one or more of the said matter and not found reasonably suitable for occupation in that condition.

SLUMS A GREAT DANGER TO THE POPULATION

J.S. Saksena and P.N. Govindarajuler in their article "Health Care For Urban Slums with special reference to Bangalore City" have rightly sensed the problem. To quote them:

> "Slum-dwellers have the worst of both the worlds-urban and rural. On one side they suffer from economic hardships, lack of education and absence of health infrastructure like the rural population. On the other hand, they also suffer the ill-effects of over-crowding, pollution and rootlessness characteristic of large metropolitan cities".

They further add that: "Most comforts and conveniences of the cities are sustained by the work done by slum-dwellers. As such, the affluent and the privileged have the moral responsibility to try to mitigate and alleviate their suffering. Rural population may be ignorant of the "goodies" they are missing, but a slum-dweller is painfully aware of the privations suffered by him due to his constantly rubbing shoulders with urban affluence and conspicuous consumption with resultant resentment."[4]

GROWTH AND EXTENT OF SLUMS

Provisional data relating to slums in the 2001 Census throw some interesting light on the slum population. Nearly 28 million persons lived in the slums in 1981, accounting for 17.5 per cent of the urban population. The estimates for 1991 were 45.7 million slum dwellers accounting for 21.5 per cent of population. According to the 2001 Census, there are 40.6 million persons living in slums in 607 towns/cities, and they account for 22.8 per cent of the population of these cities. However, the latest Census data also reflect the problems inherent in not having an accepted definition of slums and absence of proper listing of slum settlements in the urban offices concerned with slum improvement and civic amenities. The practice of notifying slums under relevant laws is not being followed, especially where the land involved belongs to Government or any of its agencies. As a result of these lacunae, these data are not definitive because towns with less than 50,000 population, and slum clusters, which are not formally or informally recognized if the population was less than 300 are excluded.

While demographic data on slum populations and on civic amenities to slum dwellers from the Census are still awaited, there appears to be no change in the basic level or improvement in the features of slum settlements despite several decades of programmes for the environmental improvement and upgradation of slums. There is cause to wonder whether 'Cities without Slums' is a slogan about an objective, which, however desirable, is believed to be unreachable, or whether it is a serious planning and urban development concern. Certainly the degree of effort to upgrade slums to a more habitable level does not indicate a serious effort in this direction.[5]

GROWTH OF SLUMS

Slums by and large are the creation of urbanization process, which necessitates the transfer of rural poverty to urban environment. Lack of resources with the local level agencies results in non-provision of basic services and accordingly large number of slums grow in cities. Percentage of population of slums increases in direct proportion to the population and size of the city of which they form part. Larger cities have more proportion of population in slums.

World Development Report of 1994 prepared by the World Bank says that growth of slums in India is primarily due to inadequate infrastructures. It further says that though proportion of population living below the poverty line has shown a decline, number of people living in slums have, however, increased. Thus, growth of slums cannot be visualized as the product of poverty alone; infact numbers of other factors are responsible for the growth of slums. Government of India has launched a new scheme to prevent the growth of slums in urban areas. New Scheme provides alternative sites to existing slum-dwellers/EWS Families living in cities with population ranging between 5 to 20 lacs. House sites are allotted on a graded scale of 35 sq. mts., for cities in population range between 5-10 lacs, 30 sq. mts, for population ranges between 15-20 lacs. However, scheme does not provide for slums in cities dwellers belonging to EWS category with special emphasis on people below poverty line. These schemes are operational in few selected towns.

Growths of slums have become faster over the years and this problem has spread over all the settlements. Major problem in solving shelter-related issues of EWS or shelterless is the availability of land. It is proposed to create a Land Bank for the poor in all the urban areas, which would be funded by various financial institutions like HUDCO and other State level agencies. Further addition would be made to the Land Bank through the mechanism of earmarking 5% of total land developed under any scheme for EWS housing, which would be transferred to the Land Bank. Private colonizers would also contribute to the Land Bank. Similarly, all Town Development Schemes would earmark 5% of area for EWS housing. Thus, a large land pool would be created, which can be used for providing shelter to EWS.

The number and population of slums are always on the increase. Even many areas, in urban towns, have become so congested and short of basic services, that we can also call them slums. Life in these areas is miserable. If one has to visit old areas of Delhi, Ludhiana, Patiala, Calcutta, Bombay, for that matter, one finds that these are nothing but slums.

Let us now mention about the growth of slums in the newly planned City beautiful, i.e. Chandigarh.

The city was planned on modern lines, has also been engulfed by slums, causing misery to the slum-dwellers as well as neighbouring population. Slums or so-called bastis are increasing at a fast rate. These bastis have become a danger to the inhabitants as well as to the residents of the city. Personal observations reveal the disgusting, pathetic and painful sights. Human beings are living like animals and these bastis are potential source of epidemics, malaria and other communicable diseases. Those responsible for crating these slums should be severely punished. If this is the state of affairs of a modern city, then what would be the condition of slums in Delhi, Bombay, Calcutta, Hyderabad and so on.

A survey was conducted by the Center for Indian Development Studies, for Municipal Corporation, Chandigarh, for the implementation of the Swarn Jayanti Shahari Rozgar Yojna (SJSRY) in the city, in 37 colonies of Chandigarh, of which 23 fall in the category of rehabilitated and 14 unauthorized ones on the government land, reveals that shortage of water, slushy conditions, lack of sanitation and drainage system, especially in unauthorized colonies, are the major problems ailing them.

We must take bold steps to save the city by providing alternate sites to the existing bastis and ban the creation of future slums.

LIFE OF PEOPLE IN SLUMS

A Survey on the health status of adolescent girls in Patiala, carried out by a team of expert lady doctors, has revealed that 92.5 per cent of girls in urban slums are anemic while the percentage of such girls in urban areas is 88.6 and 86% in rural areas. It was further found that 38.7 percent girls in urban slums were severely anemic.

Not only mental disorders but problems relating to physical abuse (15.2%), domestic violence (30.2%) and sexual abuse (10.2%) were seen in urban slums indicating poverty, illiteracy and low status of women in this category.[6]

It is paradoxical situation that on the one hand they provide all services to urban population on the other, they cannot meet their needs.

Over a period of time, slum-dwellers are beginning to see themselves as citizens contributing to the economy and, therefore, deserving their own place in the sun. It is the slum and pavement dweller, who provides the vast network of services that the middle and upper classes enjoy at cheap rates. These services include the entire food supply network (vegetables, milk, eggs, butter, bread, meat, poultry as well as restaurant services), clothing, laundry, vending and sales, transport, conservancy, communication, construction and domestic services for homes, offices. The slum-dwellers, if united, have the power to bring to a halt the entire urban system, so powerful is their role in urban economy.[7]

Most of the slum-dwellers are immigrants of villages or towns and then migrate to slums or another form of low-income urban housing. They move to the place after the migrant has established himself in the city with a job, a network of friends and some sort of understanding of the political and bureaucratic structure of the municipality. However, this pattern of movement from rural to slum is a very common one. Some move permanently. This usually happens when a migrant already has a well-establishment network of relatives and friends living there. Some of migrants come not only from rural areas but also from other urban centres of the country. Others never settle permanently in the city but stay only long enough to take advantage of the economic opportunities available there before returning to their place of origin.[8]

Within the existing broad loose definition, following housing areas can be categorized as "Slum":

(i) Inner city blighted areas;
(ii) Squatter settlements on both private and public land;
(iii) Illegal land sub-divisions (unauthorized colonies);
(iv) Urban villages;
(v) Resettlement colonies (like those in Delhi); and
(vi) A squatter settlement improved under the environmental improvement scheme.[9]

SOME CASE STUDIES IN SLUMS

In Ludhiana, a woman named Geeta about 20 years has four children. She got married at the age of 14. Her husband, a Rickshaw puller earns merely Rs. 30 per day i.e. 600 per month, which he spends in drinking, smoking and gambling. Geeta woks as maid in some houses leaving her children back, earning about 1500 per month. She has one room jhuggi with no privacy. Children are being neglected. She feels exhausted and tired of life.

In Jalandhar, a woman named Sarita about 23 years age old having three children was abandoned by her husband, as he got illicit relations with her sister who was living with them. She works as a rag picker hardly making both ends meet. She feels to commit suicide but because of children. She is pulling her life.

In another case in Patiala, a woman about 25, with pale face and a mother of four children was suffering from HIV positive. Her husband alongwith his friends used to drink at night and all of them used to exploit her sexually. Her life has become miserable. She feels suffocated and cannot look after the children.

In another case in Ropar a man aged 50 has been living for the last 20 years with 3 children and his wife in small 2 rooms. Some persons in the area forced him to sell her daughters aged 13 and 15 to some persons aged 45 and 47.

He resisted but could not do anything. He complained to the Police but no case was registered. He is feeling guilty and disheartened.

An observation and case studies into the lives of people inhabiting slum areas reveal a pathetic scene, where it is difficult to watch horrible problems of people. These problems relate to the following areas:

1. Poverty.
2. Social evils like drinking, smoking, gambling, prostitution etc.
3. Poor Health—Woman mostly anemiec, Children under developed, frequent pregnancies, poor health services.
4. Illiteracy—Lack of education facilities, mostly illiterate.
5. Exploitation of women—Very low status of women, marriage mostly at the ages of 13-14-15, number of children high ranging from 3-5, works both for domestic services as well as maids to earn some money.
6. Poor Housing—Causing tensions, lack of privacy, lack of safety of young girls etc.
7. Lack of sanitation—Causing diseases and poor life.
8. Lack of potable water—They even do not get good waster to drink causing many water borne diseases.
9. Poor Environment—The all around environment has been poor causing many health problems.

LACK OF POTABLE WATER/CIVIC AMENITIES

We have seen that people in urban areas living in slums or slums like places are faced with a large number of problems concerning their life. How to over come them? How to provide good life to them? What should be done to provide them basic facilities needed for human beings? What has been the role of Government, NGOs and other agencies in providing them good life? The answer to these questions is simple i.e. People living in these areas need to come together,

TABLE 2.1

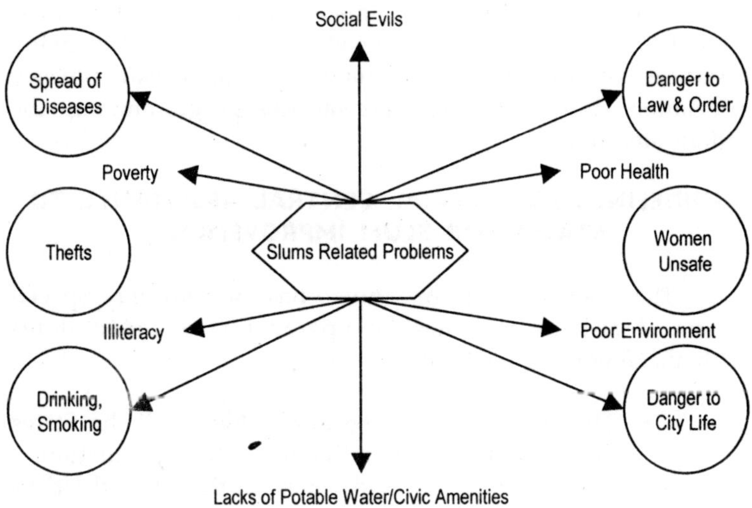

to locate problems, find solutions and put them into action with the support of municipal bodies. This is known as urban participatory development. It is based on the premises that people both men and women and especially women, have the potentiality to solve their problems.

ROLE OF THE GOVERNMENT IN IMPROVING SLUMS

Various Central Government schemes—National Slum Development Programme (NSDP), Swarna Jayanti Shahri Rozgar Yojana (SJSRY), VAMBAY, Night Shelters, Two Million Housing Scheme, Accelerated Urban Water Supply Programme (AUWSP), Low-Cost Sanitation—provide for a wide range of services to the urban poor including slum-dwellers. They include identification of the urban poor, formation of community groups, involvement of non-government organizations (NGOs), self-help/thrift and credit activities, training for livelihood, credit and subsidy for economic activities, housing and sanitation, environmental improvement, community assets, wage employment, convergence of services, etc. What is needed is to ensure that the task of meeting the needs of the slum-dwellers is better organized and effectively administered, and duly monitored at both State and Central levels. There are also many instances of successful implementation of urban poverty alleviation/slum upgrading and services programmes in the Indian situation.

GUIDELINES FOR SPECIAL CENTRAL ASSISTANCE TO STATES FOR SLUM IMPROVEMENT

The Government of India has introduced Special Central Assistance to States for upgradation of urban slums with the following elements:

- The scheme should be applicable to all the States and Union Territories having urban population.
- Funds are allocated to States on the basis of Urban slum population.

Components

- Physical amenities (water supply, storm water drains, street lights, etc.)
- Community Infrastructure centres for pre-school education, non-formal education, primary health care center, etc.
- Social Amenities like Pre-school education, non-formal education, adult education, maternity, child health, etc.
- Convergence between schemes being implemented by different line departments.
- Shelter upgradation or construction of new houses (including EWS) with minimum 10% of the allocation to States.
- State specific schemes for housing construction/ upgradation with a mix of subsidy and loan component, sanctioned in a State level project Committee with one representative from the Department of UEPA, which is the nodal Department for this scheme in the GOI.

The focus is on community infrastructure, provision of shelter, and empowerment of urban poor women, training, skill up-gradation and advocacy and involvement of NGOs, CBOs, Private institutions and other bodies. The scheme is applicable to all the States and Union Territories having urban population.

At the national level, Ministry of Urban Affairs and Employment is the nodal Ministry to monitor this programme.

The Planning Commission in the beginning of each financial year allocates funds under this scheme and Department of Expenditure releases Additional Central Assistance to States/UTs.[10]

THE IMPORTANCE OF SLUM UPGRADING

Action taken so far for slum improvement or in situ upgrading is inadequate. Re-designing and re-constructing settlements with the participation of residents and assistance from public bodies is a viable option with the least amount of disturbance to the settlers or their livelihood. This method of slum improvement needs to be practised on a much wider scale. The VAMBAY project permits in situ upgradation, and it is necessary that an early decision is taken regarding land on which slums are situated in order to facilitate upgradation.[11]

ROLE OF URBAN LOCAL GOVERNMENT—NATIONAL SLUM POLICY PRESCRIBES THE FOLLOWING ROLE FOR LOCAL SELF-GOVERNMENT

Planning for Integration

(a) Modify Existing Planning Framework

All existing planning instruments such as Master Plans. Land Use Plans etc should be modified to ensure that slums and informal settlements can be properly integrated into the wider urban areas. In order to achieve this objective, it will be necessary to:

(i) Ensure that all Master Plans and Land Use plans allow for **high density; mixed use** (for micro-enterprise) land occupation in all slums/informal settlements. This will ensure that every ULB designates sufficient and more appropriate (higher density lower cost) living and working space of the urban poor within the urban area.

(ii) Master Plans and Land Use Plans should also ensure that all new land development schemes make sufficient provision for land to house low income workers as required by such schemes.

(iii) All plans and other regulatory instruments must provide sufficient flexibility to modify layouts and building regulations in line with more realistic density/mixed use requirements.

The powers to implement such changes outlined in (i) to (iii) above should be vested in the ULBs, within parameters laid down by State governments.

(a) Integrated Municipal Development Plan (IMDP)

All ULBs should begin to work towards the formulation of an Integrated Municipal Development Plan. The principle objective of this plan is to ensure that the ULB has an adequate and sustainable level of infrastructure and services for all its residents and that such infrastructure and services and planned and delivered in an equitable manner. In order to achieve this objective it will be necessary to identify the capital and recurrent requirements and costs for the city as a whole (eg. Bulk water supply) as well as the specific wards and neighbourhood within the city (secondary and tertiary water supply). The plan should prioritize ways and means of narrowing the gap between the better-serviced and less well serviced (slums) areas of the ULB.

(b) Convergence

The IMDP process assumes the implementation of the 74th Amendment and embodies the principle of convergence of activities and funds to achieve more efficient and equitable urban development. The IMDP will incorporate existing plans and reflect schemes and budget allocations as follows:

- Master Plans/Land Use Plans and other statutory instruments.
- Urban Development Plans and Schemes.
- Urban Poverty Alleviation Plans and Schemes.
- Department Plans and Schemes in the ULB area.

(a) Dynamic Multi-Year Planning

The IMDP, outlined in (b) above, should be undertaken as a dynamic process which will be updated and reviewed every three years. The overall plan should then be implemented through Annual Action Plans and budget allocations so that development work can be taken up in a phased manner. These Annual Action Plans should reflect plan priorities based on the level of service deprivation or service gaps pertaining in the wards and neighbourhood.

(b) Bottom Up Planning

Planning should begin at the micro-level with each urban poor area drawing up a list of existing services and identifying gaps and deficiencies. This activity should be undertaken by the community using participatory planning techniques and each plan should include a clear prioritization of needs and an indication of different stakeholder contributions towards costs. ULBs will be required to submit evidence of community participation in planning service provision.

8. Environmental Improvement

The provision of physical infrastructure components such as water supply, drainage, sanitation, improved access, electricity etc. should support the ultimate objective of improved quality of life. The evidence from existing slum improvement projects clearly shows that an improved physical environment greatly facilitates the integration of the settlement in the wider urban area and at the same time, contributes to improved livelihoods and health and well being of the community.

(a) Approach

(i) Community Based Approach

All physical upgrading and improvement in informal settlements should adopt a Community Based Approach with the active involvement of members of the community at every stage of design, implementation, and maintenance of services and assets. Community structures and systems should reflect local conditions and preferences rather than conform to any uniform pattern. Communities have an important role to play at all stages of service delivery in terms of location of the service points, day-to-day functioning of the service and guarding against its misuse. Communities should be encouraged to contribute land and resources to help establish community centres and to promote the collection of user charges to contribute to the operation of certain services.

(ii) Target Women and Children

There is a need to target women and children directly in the design and implementation of physical infrastructure and the delivery of social and economic services. Infrastructure users, especially the urban poor and women are central to the sustainability of any investment decisions related to infrastructure.

(iii) Service Delivery on Individual Household Basis

Wherever possible, the delivery of basic services such as water, sanitation and electricity should be provided on an individual household basis and may even precede the granting of full tenure rights. Individual connections will improve operations, maintenance, and facilitate recovery of user charges and thus improve the overall environment.

(iv) Contracting-out

Wherever possible works should be undertaken by communities/CBOs under appropriate supervision of ULBs. Such works must be done according to departmental norms and procedures with proper muster rolls maintained and other stipulations to be observed. Services may also be contracted out, where appropriate, to NGOs and other private companies. Solid waste management has already been successfully contracted-out by many ULBs. Similarly, the maintenance of pay and use toilets has also been contracted-out to NGOs and community based organizations (CBOs). State enactments/procedures dealing with improvement works should be modified to allow the implementation of such works to be undertaken on a contract basis by the community/CBOs.

(b) Physical Infrastructure Development

The guiding principle and expected outcomes to be kept in focus while planning and implementing the following basic infrastructure and services are outlined as:

(i) Water Supply

Quantum, duration, timing and water quality are the four critical factors in planning water supply delivery. Dual and standby systems, such as piped supply supported by local hand-pumps should be considered as a means of helping to address these four factors.

Even where individual water tap connections are provided, it may be desirable to install hand-pumps or community storage facilities to offset poor frequency of supply and inadequate storage capacity at individual household level.

(ii) Sanitation

ULBs should avoid constructing community latrines within slum/informal settlements as these quickly degenerate on account of poor operations and maintenance (O & M) thus becoming counter productive to public health. Where there is insufficient space for individual sanitation options (mostly where on-site disposal systems have to be adopted) groups or cluster latrines with clearly demarcated and agreed household responsibilities for O & M may be a suitable alternative option.

It is vital that any community wide sanitation programme be preceded by an awareness campaign designed to raise demand for the implementation of specific sanitation options. This would greatly facilitate all subsequent O & M, activities as would also assist the process of raising financial contributions. Many members of the community, especially male members, do not perceive sanitation, as a clear priority need. This needs to be addressed before embarking upon the installation of sanitation.

Considering the limitations on improving sanitation in many towns due to absence of underground drainage and sewerage systems, low cost sanitation options, particularly twin pit pour flush latrines may be a more appropriate and cost effective option for slums duly keeping environmental safeguards in mind. Efforts should be made to popularize and facilitate the introduction of such systems wherever appropriate. The tenurial status and likelihood of a settlement getting relocated at some point in the future should not deter promoting such systems since the benefits of such environmental improvement far exceed the initial investment incurred.

(iii) Pedestrian and Vehicular Access Ways

Paved access for pedestrians and/or vehicles will greatly improve overall accessibility. Paved access will encourage investment in the community and promote physical integration with neighbouring areas. It may also help to improve social integration within between communities. Paved access will also greatly facilitate the introduction of other related infrastructure such as storm water drains, underground drainage water supply, electricity and collection/removal of garbage. Paving would also help in maintaining a clean environment and help reduce flooding and water stagnation. Paved access ways also facilitates the use of such facilities for social activity, extension of household activities and space for economic activity.

(iv) Storm Water Drains

Drains in slums serve the dual purpose of carrying sullage water from individual houses as well as draining storm water. It is crucial to integrate the outfalls of such drains with the city's main drainage system. The planning of slum drainage should be fully integrated into the planning of neighbouring systems as well as the city as a whole.

(v) Electricity

Individual house connections will greatly enhance the comfort and safety of living and working conditions for residents. The mere provision of street lighting without formal household connections leads to illegal tapping and loss of revenue and at the same time causes unplanned loading of the system and fire hazards. Community management systems for collection of user charges will facilitate improved revenue recovery and reduce revenue losses.

(vi) Solid Waste Collection

Sustained awareness campaigns and provision of waste collection receptacles will facilitate a clearner environment. Urban Local Bodies could organize 'clean slum competitions' and institute prizes to create more awareness and encourage the community groups to maintain a clean environment within their localities. At community level, management systems that employ private sweepers by collecting monthly charges may also be adopted.

9. Improving Access to Social Services

Basic services of health, education and access to credit are crucial for human capital development and reduce the incidence of poverty. Improved access to social services would also help building up the capacities of poor and empowering them to improve their own living conditions and quality of life. Effective delivery of these services would also reduce social inequities and promote integration of people residing in slums into the social and economic networks of the city as a whole, thereby enhancing the overall productivity of the city. Various physical infrastructure components such as water supply and sanitation have a direct bearing on improving health conditions in slums. This section outlines a number of complementary services where ULBs should actively seek to improve access for the urban poor.

METHODS OF SLUM IMPROVEMENT

There is a continuous tug-of-war between city level authorities and the slum-dwellers and the battle line is continuously redrawn in the form of regularization of unauthorized colonies. This causes considerable stress on the city administration including law and order problems leading to considerable costs and inconvenience to the city population as a whole. In many cases, such unauthorized colonies are demolished or upgraded incurring huge costs. The city authorities undertake a sort of fire-fighting salvage operation from time to time incurring large expenditure. This cost is estimated to be many times more than the cost involved in habitating them by proper planning by reserving pre-planned land for this group of population. Past experience indicates that no amount of legal and regulatory mechanisms could stop movement of people in search of economic upliftment. What, therefore, is there to be done? More specifically, what our local governments do? Never in the history have there been such large urban agglomerations. Future emphasis must be on working out ways and means for interdependence between national and local units and between local governments with one another. It is realized that the solutions to slum-dwellers' problems can be found together with them.[12]

It is worthwhile to examine how our governments, specifically the urban local governments are dealing with this situation after five decade. The growth of slum population in these growing cities is so prolific that, our local governments have lost control of the deteriorating urban decay. In other words, the government organizations have generally found themselves largely ineffective to forge authentic partnership with the urban slum people in solving habitat related issues.[13]

I. Legislative Support

Legislative supports for slum improvement has been provided by the Slum Areas (Improvement and Clearance) Acts adopted by various States. The operation of the improvement schemes is made possible by statutory provisions in the Slum Act in those states, where it has been passed. The Act broadly provides the following powers:

(a) Power to the competent authority to declare an area to be slum area if the buildings in that area are unfit for human inhabitants or are detrimental to the safety of health or morals.
(b) The Act empowers the competent authority to serve notice upon the owner of a building or land in a slum area, to execute the works of improvement.
(c) Power to acquire land in a slum area to execute the improvement work.
(d) Protection to tenants in slum areas from eviction.
(e) Slum Improvement Boards were to be set-up under the Act to organize, supervise the work of slum improvement in the State.

The legal definition of 'slum' places emphasis only on the physical aspects of slum. However, it does not make any mention of ownership of land or legality or illegality of structures (Bapat Meera, 1983). The definition of slum areas as enacted, in these slum areas, legalization is quite broad. However, declared slums form only 5 to 15% of the housing stock in major Indian cities. Government grants in the environmental improvement scheme are channelized only to declared slums. The declaration of slum area in this context assumes greater significance.[14]

2. Judicial Support

In a major judgment affecting at least 30 lakhs people living in the Capital's slums, the Supreme Court has asked the authorities concerned to remove their shelters and stop further growth of unauthorized hutments on public land. It also asked the civic authorities to comply with the 10 directives, which are aimed at providing better hygiene, clean environment and ensuring that "the Capital of the biggest democracy in the world is not branded as being one of the most polluted cities in the World".

Passing strictures on the civic authorities, the court said: "Tolerating filth, while not taking action against the lethargic and inefficient work force for fear of annoying them, is un-understandable and impermissible". "The employees", the judges said, "were perhaps sanguine in their belief that non-performance is not frowned upon by the government or by the head of organization and no harm will befall them".

On the mushrooming growth of the slums, the court said, "establishment or creating of slums, it seems, appears to be good business and is well organized. Large areas of public land, in this way, are usurped for private use free of cost. It is difficult to believe that this can happen in the Capital without passive or active connivance of the land owning agencies and/or the municipal authorities."

3. Urban Community Development Approach

Slum Improvement under the urban community development programme in Hyderabad, primarily aims at organizing the community and to articulate and achieve the felt needs. One of the notable features of UCD programme has been granting of tenure to slum-dwellers by rehousing the occupants in the same area, with construction of new houses. Land tenure is granted free of cost and credit for house construction is arranged. Individual house level toilets and taps are envisaged. Efforts to extend health and nutrition programmes are also made. Nearly 20 activities affecting the overall life of people have been initiated under the urban community development.[15]

4. People's Participation

Participatory development is not an attempt to replace the top-down development approach with slum-dwellers/low income participation. Rather, it should stress the need for the government participation in terms of national-level economic planning and coordination of development planning and the demerits of widening disparities and worsening poverty inherent in slum dwellers. Participatory development attempts to introduce a bottom-up style of development in order to remedy the government approach's shortcomings, specifically by focusing on qualitative improvements in slum-dwellers participation.[16]

Participation should not be temporary; it must evoke

the sustainable upgrading of participation quality. For this to happen, the basic conditions should be met to facilitate the long-term process of participation and its self-reliant sustainability. A long-term process of participation mentioned here is: raising the awareness of slum-dwellers, forming community groups among them, upgrading their requisite resource management abilities, creating norms or internalizing their mechanisms and improving capabilities for external negotiations. To achieve the above-mentioned goal, we need a long-term vision, willingness to improve and support from NGO's to train leaders.[17]

Participation of slum-dwellers can reduce the cost of the social programme, which government often invests. It will give an idea to the government with a great deal of information on the social and economic needs of the population. It will help the government to identify the potential leader who can assist in the development process or at least disseminate information on government goals.[18]

It is not the contention that urban development is an easy task, or that people's participation is the magic wand, which banishes all impediments with a wave and a flourish. What is being emphasized is only:

- That slum-dwellers have as much of a right as anyone else to participate in governance;
- That slum-dwellers provide invaluable services to the social and economic life of the city. Their participation in its governance should be viewed not as a condescension, but rather as a measure of enhancing the quality and experience of urban living for all;
- That, from the practical angle, through the creation of synergies and through the generation of co-operation and enthusiasm, the difficulties and obstacles that confront urban administrators have greater chance of being overcome when people's participation in governance is ensured;
- That democratically constituted, empowered Neighbourhood committees are an effective instruments towards the achievement of this objective.[19]

5. Need or Providing Education for Urban Survival

There is a growing recognition that despite the government's best efforts and intentions, the majority of households still have to fend for themselves and learn to manage their lives in a hostile environment. People will always have to sell their skills, services or goods in a private sector dominated market and negotiate to rent rooms or purchase slum huts outside the government system. Equipping people with skills to become better operators in this environment is one way in which larger number of people can be supported in their search for self-reliance. In this contest the UNDP's Urban Management Programmes proposal for development of tools to provide "Education for Urban Survival" is an interesting innovation.[20]

The slum-dwellers can be provided training in skill development. Municipal Personnel can help them in marketing their products through super bazzar etc.

6. Taxing the Beneficiaries

Most of the Services in urban slums are free of cost. The slum-dwellers can contribute in a small way, which should be tapped. This would add to the resources to make slum life better as well as create interest among slum-dwellers, when they spend their own money.

The environmental improvement scheme is based on total subsidy from the Central Government. The promise of public grants, which is a corollary to the declaration of an area as slum often encourages the inclusion of settlements belonging to middle income households also. In some cases private land has been illegally sub-divided and sold by owners to circumvent the Urban Land Ceiling Act, they managed to get the area declared as slum. The area was subsequently improved at Government cost. In such cases beneficiaries of government subsidy are certainly not the "Urban Poor". Even in squatter settlements, there are significant numbers of households, who can afford and are willing to pay for improvements, which they want. The study of popular settlements in Bhopal confirms this (Risbud, Neelima, 1987).

Resource mobilization from beneficiaries has not at all

been explored and Slum Improvement Programmes is offered as a welfare action. This has gradually shaped people's attitude of expecting everything free of cost from Government. This is further strengthened, when the politicians condone the recoveries. Credit available for improvement from Housing and Urban Development Corporation (HUDCO) and World Bank requires recovery and minimization of subsidy. In some cities all the three programmes are implemented simultaneously in different settlements (e.g. in Indore, the Environmental Improvement schemes, the HUDCO aided schemes and World Bank aided schemes, all are operative).[21]

7. Ensuing Genuine Interest and Seriousness among Planners and Policy-Markers

Urban-dwellers have become very important for politicians contesting elections. They take interest in slum-dwellers only during election time. They forget them after the elections. Programmes are formulated in a hurry without any permanent impact. This should be avoided. Slums-dwellers should ask for permanent benefits.

8. Educating the Urban Dwellers about Social and Economic Evils

A personal observation revealed that slum-dwellers, in spite of earning by all family members substantial income, still remain in the depressed poverty. A further probing revealed that the slum-dwellers are spending a substantial amount of their income on drinking, smoking, gambling, prostitution, etc. An education to stop their interest in these activities is essential. Besides, the population growth is very high in slums. There is, therefore, a need of sex and population education to limit family size.

From the foregoing, it is obvious that current programmes towards reducing urban poverty, which are expenditure-oriented, whether in the form of subsidies or capital grants in cash and kind, have more of a political dimension than economic or social goals. The last two decades have also indicated that urban poverty alleviation programmes tend to get concentrated during pre-election time and come to be used as substantial vote-catchers. Provisions of services, regularization of unauthorized constructions, allotment of land and credit for house constructions; all are in this category and can have only a short-term objective. In the long-term they lead to waste of valuable land and natural resources and even more important loss of opportunity to set right the economic inequalities, which economic growth today is giving rise to. Development of the informal sector in the urban areas specially metropolitan cities through financial, legal and resource facilities could go a long way in elevating the vulnerable sections of population to a stable level and making these sections productive components in the urban economy. The present programmes hardly aim at meeting this objective. There is no programme except perhaps extension of credit facility to a limited pupose, which has attempted to help innovative activities amongst the informal sector for which the metropolitan cities present ample opportunities.

To sum up, there is need for restructuring of urban development programmes away from capital investment and capital subsidy commitments to upgradation of the capability for self-employment, innovative enterprise, new entrepreneurship in production areas, where the equation is that of current support to be repaid by future earnings. It is the investment to be repaid by future earnings. It is the investment in insurance type of programmes rather than investments in expenditure programmes that would help eliminate urban poverty progressively over the next two decades and to this end both planned programmes as well infrastructure development should be directed.[22]

CONCLUSION

Slums are a slur on the fair name of Urban Government, State Government and the Union Government. These can be improved or improved only with sincere efforts on the part of Urban Government, Urban population and slum-dwellers.

Draft Status Population, 1995 by Government of Punjab, Department of Housing and Urban Development, Punjab.

(December 1995), suggest the following for minimizing growth of slums in urban areas.[23]

(i) Relaunching of the Integrated Urban Poverty Alleviation Scheme (IUPAS) which would include restructured existing urban poverty alleviation programmes providing for a package to urban poor.

(ii) Allocation and creation of a fund with annual contribution, for income generating activities and provision of infrastructure for urban poor.

(iii) Establishment of Urban Poverty Alleviation Fund in every municipality since slum-related issues are included in the Twelfth Schedule of 74th Constitutional Amendment Act, 1992.

(iv) Urban Shelter-related programmes would be community-based so as to involve the users in the programme.

(v) Close monitoring of all the programmes by State level agencies so as to ensure effective implementation.

(vi) Keeping close watch on the growth and development of slums and to involve appropriate strategies to minimize them.

(vii) To undertake shelter upgradation programmes for slums on priority basis and to link it with the issue of gainful employment.

(viii) Involvement of private sector and NGO's in the programme.

Temporary solutions have been tried by slum wing by providing tankers for drinking water during summer and mobile toilets, which are too meager to effect improvement. Besides, these are only interim measures, which are costlier in the longer run.[24]

The preceding paras have indicated the various alternative solutions to take care of the shelter needs of the slum settlements and each of the solutions has to be applied depending upon the prevailing situations and no one answer can be prescribed for all situations. What is required is to judiciously select the alternative and appropriate solutions depending upon the acceptability of the same to the slum-dwellers and the city development agency. Success is best achieved where there is a meeting point on the nature of solutions from the point of view of the slum-dwellers and development agency.[25]

SLUM IMPROVEMENT

Although there is a lot of talk about community participation, it is conspicuously absent in the improvement programmes, where it is most essential. The question is who wants improvement? At present, it appears that improvements are thrust on people as public works. Communities are never motivated to initiate improvement process. This makes all the difference in attitudes of the beneficiaries. This is why most of them have come to believe that it is for the public agency to do their jobs. The community plays a passive role and contributes only in terms of giving information. They are neither informed about, what is to be improved nor the cost of improvement.

Effective management of the programme is vital for efficient utilization of public and individual resources. Mostly Slum Improvement Boards merely act as channels for disbursement of grants received from Central Government. The local bodies as public works generally take up the implementation. Because the municipal bodies have so many functions to perform, the environmental improvement does not get priority. Agencies like development authority are not interested in small works of improvement. The Slum Boards are ill equipped both in terms of skills and procedures to rationally designed projects of comprehensive slum improvement.

TOWARDS A NATIONAL SLUM POLICY

The Draft National Slum Policy drawn up by the Department of Urban Employment Poverty Alleviation in the Ministry of Urban Development in April 1999, had been widely debated and many comments received. It needs to be finalized. A National Policy on slums is of great significance given the degree of wrong perception regarding the nature and extent of the slum problem. Such a policy can help bring an attitudinal change among the authorities and the people at large, including the urban poor and the slum-dwellers, regarding measures to improve their quality of life and make our cities free from the worst features of slums. Slums are generally treated as the inevitable outcome of continuing migration of unskilled labour, but, in fact, most slum-dwellers are permanent residents of the city. In many instances, families in slums span several generations. The main objectives of a slum policy would be:

- To create awareness of the underlying principles that guide the process of slum development and improvement and the options that are available for bringing about the integration of these settlements and the communities residing there with the urban area as a whole.
- To strengthen the legal and policy framework to facilitate the process of slum development and improvement on a sustainable basis; to ensure that the slum population are provided civic services, amenities, and economic opportunities to enable them to rise above the degrading conditions in which they live.
- To arrive at a policy of affirming the legal and tenurial rights of the slum-dwellers.
- To establish a framework for involving all stakeholders in the efficient and smooth implementation of policy objectives.

Focusing on slums enables planners to look beyond income levels to neighbourhood and environmental considerations and this results in a more multi-dimensional view of urban poverty. In view of the progress made in decentralized urban governance through the 74th Constitutional Amendment, it is necessary to ask how this has benefited the slum-dwellers and provided them an increased opportunity to articulate their needs and obtain assistance from civic authorities and urban planners. It does appear that the effort has been more towards providing some amount of civic services in an un-coordinated fashion than towards devising all-embracing programmes with participation of the slum-dwellers themselves, and finding solutions which provide not only a decent quality of life with prospects of further improvement, but also make slums redundant in our urban habitations. Slum dwellers need not perennially be at the receiving end of selected doles but must be made part of the urban economic and social processes with adequate opportunities for improving their lives, while contributing what is acknowledged to be a major share in the economic activities of the cities. Upgradation of living conditions of the urban poor has to be recognized as part of the national development process.

Some of the obvious lapses in slum programmes are:

- Non-listing of all habitations, big or small, which should be classified as slums.
- Lack of basic information on the number of households in such habitations, and the status of basic amenities.
- Absence of a master plan for a period of five years to gradually increase the level of civic amenities.
- Adherence to outdated and totally inadequate standards of services to the slum-dwellers, under the EIUS component.
- Failure to provide specific provisions in municipal laws for dealing with issues relating to the urban poor, slums, and economic planning for poverty alleviation, etc., which flow from the 74th Constitutional Amendment; failure to build up capacity in municipal bodies to provide the required services to slum communities and the urban poor.
- Uncertainty regarding agency arrangement for various slum improvement tasks between the municipal authority, development authority, slum board, housing board, parastatals, etc., and failure

to provide a coordinating institutional arrangement;

- Failure to implement provisions made in Comprehensive Development Plans for the housing, and economic needs (production and marketing activities) of the urban poor, especially provision of land, and facilities for street vendors and hawkers. In the absence of such planning, unplanned growth takes place leading to "informal" or unauthorized low quality settlements, and unauthorized hawking which subjects the poor to harassment from petty officials. It is often said that 'there is no place for the existing provisions are not implemented for the benefit of the urban poor.
- Failure on the part of land-owning agencies on which slums are located to take decisions on permission to make environmental improvement and in situ upgradation of slum clusters.
- Failure to converge available civic services in sanitation, paved access and drainage, streetlights, health-care, water supply, education, etc., by organizing responsibility cells and involving the beneficiaries in planning of services.
- Lack of a commitment to achieve a breakthrough in bringing slum-dwellers out of the stigma and misery of living in slums, and instead, use funds such as National Slum Development Programme for tinkering with the symptoms.[26]

SLUM OF THE MIND

At least 35 per cent of our cities live in slum settlement, and their population is increasing at more than double the general growth rate of urban population. Blinkered policies of the past have created nightmarish conditions in Indian cities. Unless we change the contours of our mindscape the urban landscape will continue to decay.

The maladies that afflict India's cities are not merely localized wounds that can be cleaned, disinfected and healed;

they have deep roots. Basically the problem is civilizational. Cities shape civilization and are in turn shaped by them. It is impossible to view them separately.[27]

Despite all the efforts being taken by the departments in providing housing and basic civic amenities to the urban poor living in the slum areas, the population in these areas has increased. As is evident from a census report for the town of Bombay. The report says:

> "Preliminary findings of the state government's ongoing census on slums in Mumbai suggest that the city's slum population has doubled over the last five years. Officials concerned with the census say that over 60 lakh slum-dwellers have been enumerated against the 40 lakh recorded when the census was last updated in 1995."[28]

Service required by the urban poor-physical infrastructure as well as human development services—are simple to enumerate and, over the years, most of them have been attempted at least in a rudimentary fashion. During the Tenth Plan, the focus has to be on upgrading these services, and on convergence for achieving synergy. Convergence of services, such as water supply, drainage, solid waste management, as well as for health care, family welfare, education, anganwadis and creches should be the main plank of urban poverty alleviation. Outlays on water supply and sanitation should, in particular, focus on the needs of the urban poor. Setting up basic health and education units such as creches, anganwadis, primary schools, public health units and primary health centres (PHCs) in areas where the urban poor live is equally important.

At the state level there is a need to:

- Set up urban poverty and slum improvement task forces. The first task should be to upscale the old standards of services under EIUS and make them more relevant to the average level of services available to the residents of the town/city.
- City administration should create urban poverty

alleviation (UPA) cells at the municipal level. The cell should have representation of all the services required by slum-dwellers, as well as of the Community Development Societies set up under SJSRY, and NGOs active in the field. The UPA cell should be in overall charge of urban poverty and slum related programmes.

- The UPA cells should draw up City Poverty Alleviation Plans in which the community organizations of the poor created under the Swarn Jayanti Shahri Rozgar Yojana (SJSRY) should be involved. The tasks of various agencies should be well-defined and coordination should be effective. The thrust should be on the provision of all basic services such as potable water and sanitation services, including household taps, toilets with septic tanks, covered drains, waste collection services etc. to the slum settlements. Other activities for the socio-economic up-liftment of the slum populations should also be taken up, making maximum use of the SJSRY and similar schemes.
- Citywide master plans for slum improvement should be drawn up with the objective of removing the slum characteristics of the selected settlements. The annual programmes and projects, including those to be financed out of NSDP funds, should be based on such master plans.

Programmes for urban infrastructure supported by the Central Government, such as the IDSMT and the Mega City Scheme should have adequate provisions for meeting the infrastructural deficiencies of settlements of the urban poor.[29]

MONITORING AND EVALUATION—ACTION POINTS

As stated in National Draft Slum Policy, each intervention, programme or project under this policy shall need a monitoring and evaluation mechanism. Based on the guiding principles given above, key points necessary to design and build effective monitoring and evaluation into various projects of strategic interventions for achieving the objectives of the National Slum Policy are given as under:-

- Monitoring and evaluation should be built into every programme and its management from the beginning in terms of clear responsibilities and budgets.
- Ensure that procedures and conditions are connected to the results of monitoring and evaluation.
- Try to ensure that monitoring and credible bodies carry out evaluation. These may include both the communities' affected themselves and independent third parties.
- Monitoring and evaluation should allow both immediate feedback to action and more considered reflection and response.
- Monitoring should be frequent in the early stages, but requires follow up over an extended period until the desired and acceptable levels of project programme objectives are achieved.

Urban slums are a slur on the face of the modern civilization. There is a need to help the slum dwellers to lead a decent life since they are doing a lot for the development of the city.

Notes and References

1. Puri, K.K., 'Urbanization and Slums: A Dimensional Analysis', in "Revamping Urban Governments in India" edited by Dr. Pardeep Sachdeva, New Delhi, Kitab Mahal, p. 43.
2. Sanganal, Ashok, 'Participation of Slum Dwellers in Urban Governance', Shelter, Vol. III, No. 1, p. 35.
3. Gurumukhi, K.T., 'Slum Releated Policies and Programmes', Shelter, Vol. 3, No. 2, April 2000, pp. 57-58.
4. Goel, S.L., 'Planning and Administration of Urban Basic Services: A Case Study of Una (H.P.)' in 'Development Planning and Administration', Ed. S. Bhatnagar and S.L. Goel, pp. 167-168.
5. Government of India, Planning Commission, 'Tenth Five Year Plan (2002-2007)', Volume II, Sectoral Policies and Programmes, pp. 627-628.

6. The Hindustan Times, 24 December 1999.
7. Shelter, Vol. III, No. 1, p. 35.
8. *Ibid.*, p. 42.
9. Risbud, Neelima, 'Slum Improvement in India—Some Issues', Delhi Vikas Patra, p. 27.
10. Annual Report, 2002-2003, Ministry of Urban Affairs and Employment, Government of India.
11. Government of India, Planning Commission, 'Tenth Five Year Plan (2002-2007)', Volume II, Sectoral Policies and Programmes, p. 629.
12. Shetler, Vol. VIII, No. 1, pp. 36-37.
13. *Ibid.*, p. 36.
14. Risbud, Neelima, 'Slum Improvement Policies in India - Some Issues', Delhi Vikas Patra, pp. 25-26.
15. *Ibid.*, p. 6.
16. Shelter, Vol. III,No. 1, p. 43.
17. *Ibid.*, p. 43.
18. *Ibid.*, p. 44.
19. *Ibid.*, p. 49.
20. 'Urban India in Crisis', Edited by Kulwant Singh, p. 188.
21. Risbud, Neelima, Delhi, Vikas Patra, p. 28.
22. 'Development Programmes for Urban Poor', Edited by Grish K. Mishra and M.K. Narain, pp. 69-70.
23. 'Urban Development Strategy for Punjab', 'Draft Status Report, 1995', Department of Housing and Urban Development, Government of Punjab, pp. 29-30.
24. Shelter, Vol., I, No. 3, p. 16.
25. *Ibid.*, p. 9.
26. Government of India, Planning Commission, 'Tenth Five Year Plan (2002-2007)', Volume II, Sectoral Policies and Programmes, pp. 628-629.
27. Jagmohan, Union Minister for Urban Development, Government of India, 'Slum of the Mind', India Today, January 31, 2000, p. 48
28. Indian Express, Chandigarh, Dated 7 November 2000.
29. Government of India, Planning Commission, 'Tenth Five Year Plan (2002-2007)', Volume II, Sectoral Policies and Programmes, p. 629.

3

Participatory Development through Community-based Structures

An analysis of the programmes aimed at improvement of standard of living of slum dwellers during the last three decade through different programmes of the Government Administrated through urban local bodies revealed that there has not been difference in the lives of slum dwellers? What is the reason? What alternative model can be adopted? The answer is the need of the slum dwellers working together under the guidance of experts available with urban local bodies for improving their status. This means that slum dwellers must not depend wholly on Government but must take interest in their own welfare. In this way slum dwellers can move from self-dependence to self-reliance. They may follow the pro-verb, "God helps those who help themselves". Our Politicians and municipal authorities have been assuring them of doing a lot for them but these are only promises. Slum dwellers have the potentiality and can improve their lives provided they take part in their own welfare. This is not true of developing countries only but equally apply to developed world. Municipal Finances, all the world over are limited. These can be supplemented by the co-operation of beneficiaries. Just to illustrate some examples from developed & developing countries.

The most widespread services administered by the municipalities of great cites are public health, hospitals, city planning, water supply, sewerage and sewage disposal, public cleansing, education, highway construction, street maintenance and lighting, public assistance, welfare, police forces, fire fighting, the provision of public housing and housing regulation, parks and playgrounds, recreational and cultural amenities, public transport, markets, abattoirs, cemeteries and crematoria. These services form the central core of local government, although all of them are not everywhere entrusted to the municipal government of the great city.[1]

Arne F. Leemans in his Article on "Amsterdam" stated:

> "It is undeniable that several services do not meet the desired quality, nor are they available in sufficient quantity. It has already been noted that severe financial limitations form the principal reason for the lag in municipal services, and also affect their quality. A striking example is offered by the plan for the 'new town', Bijlermeer. It is likely that his imaginative plan will not be fully implemented in the way originally envisaged since central government will only provide financial support for housing projects if expenses are reduced to the standards it has set for low cost housing. As a result, the city government will probably have to resort mainly to traditional patterns of town planning and housing methods.

Another limitation that hampers the city government in drawing up and executing plans is the lack of space. Large-scale slum clearance and urban renewal have been impeded by the fact that no ground was available to the city government for new housing, thus making it impossible to provide houses for people displaced from the clearance areas."[2]

Fouad D. Alided-Tawal in his Article on "Cairo" stated:

> "Cairo had been centrally governed till the Local Government Law was promulgated in 1960. The

> governing council has undertaken the responsibility of establishing and managing the different local services as well as the district councils, which carry on local affairs aiming at the welfare of the citizens. Through the two-tier structure, the inhabitants of the city have the chance to make known their wishes and wants, for the lower tier is in a position to know more bout the people's needs. Such a system has increased the people's participation. Now they play a positive role in carrying out the resolutions decided by the councils."

The new system has been faced with accumulated problems, particularly the rapid growth of population. Despite the great efforts exerted by the city to provide the citizens with necessary services these are still inadequate. There is a shortage of housing, although thousands of low cost dwellings were erected. Transportation, though the streets are crowded with various means of transport, is inadequate.[3]

Ali Ashraf and Hestile Green in their articles on Calcutta feels that:

> "In spite of its awesome size, its wealth and hustling activity, its vital significance in the national and regional economy, Calcutta is a city in crisis. All who live in this metropolitan complex have daily experience of its characteristic problems: chronic deficits in basic utilities such as water supply, sewerage and drainage; and in community facilities such as schools, hospitals, parks and recreation spaces; severe unemployment and under-employment; congested and inadequate transportation; vast housing shortages and proliferating slum areas."[4]

Alihijit Datta and J.N. Khosla in their article on "Delhi" feel that:

> "The master plan, and especially its implementation during the last five years, seems totally inadequate to grapple firmly with problems like slum clearance and

housing, water supply, and transportation. The backlog with respect to housing has increased as compared to the position when the plan was prepared, primarily because of the tremendous rate of population growth of Delhi and also due to the feeble housing programme in practice. The search for an adequate source of water supply has been equally futile, both within Delhi and also in the adjoining states. An efficient system of mass transportation is yet to come about in the shape of either a ring railway or an underground variant of it."[5]

URBAN DEVELOPMENT

The Status of Urban Local Bodies

The Constitution (74th) Amendment Act, 1992 was intended to give a more focused thrust to decentralization and the creation of a democratic governance structure with local responsibilities being assumed and managed at the local level. It was to address the inadequacies of the existing system to municipalities, redefine the relationship between the states and municipal bodies and lay the foundations of a new approach to urban management and governance that could fulfill the needs and aspirations of urban residents for development. Article 243W of the Act mandated the setting up of elected municipalities—urban local bodies (ULBs)—as the 'institutions of self government'. The important features of the Act are well-known but bear repetition since all of them have not been acted upon. These are:

- Regular elections under the supervision of the state Election Commission.
- A clear tenure of five years for the elected body;
- Protection for the elected body against arbitrary dissolution;
- Constitution of Wards Committees for greater proximity to the citizens;
- Mandate to state legislature to endow the ULBs with such powers and authority as may be necessary to enable them to function as 'institutions of self-government';

- The Twelfth Schedule which illustrates the range of responsibilities to be given to the ULB;
- The constitution of State Finance Commissions (SFCs) to review municipal finances and make recommendations regarding distribution of the proceeds of state-level taxes between the state governments and the ULBs, criteria for grants-in-aid, measures needed to improve the financial position of the municipal bodies, etc;
- Setting up District Planning Committees and Metropolitan Planning Committees for integrated as well as coordinated planning for urban and rural areas by the various agencies involved in providing civic, transport, economic and social services.

It is significant that apart from the traditional municipal functions, Article 243W allocates to ULBs the function of 'preparation of plans for economic development and social justice', and the Twelfth Schedule contains 'urban poverty alleviation' as a municipal responsibility. These take municipal bodies from being mere providers of civic amenities to a much wider arena of action encompassing economic and social planning. The Constitutional amendment has designed the ULBs as comprehensive institutions of urban self-government, and has left the details to be worked out by the state legislatures.[6]

The challenge to be met in the Tenth Plan period is to assist these elected bodies to grow organically to fulfill the demands of urban residents for a quality of life in line with world standards. Thee is no doubt that the urban governance will progressively be managed at the local level ensuring better opportunities for people to express their needs and expectations, and with professional competence and capacity supplementing the democratic nature of the ULBs. The credit for this goes to the 74th Constitutional amendment, though it has been the subject of much debate from the outset.[7]

The community structures created under SJSRY need to be strengthened and further diversified. One method would be to form associations of specific groups such as street vendors, who could have their own self-help groups, and network to create a financial interface with the formal sector financial institutions in order to gain access to credit. Social security benefits would be another area to cover. During the Tenth Plan, the scope of SJSRY should be expanded to include a scheme of contributory social security assistance sickness, disability, and old age benefits to members of the community structures, in which there will be a matching contribution from the Government.[8]

The following services can be taken through Participatory Development:

(a) Health Services

Wherever health services and national health programmes have been devolved to city level following the 74th Amendment, ULBs must build health management capacities to improve service delivery to the poor:

(i) Participatory Health Delivery

All primitive, preventive and curative health services for the urban poor should be implemented on a participatory basis with active community involvement and support. All required training and basic infrastructure should be arranged through convergence with departmental schemes.

(ii) Demand for Health Services

The community should be mobilized to create demand for better preventive health services and to access these services in a more effective manner. Hygiene behaviour changes should be promoted as an integral part of the sanitation services outlined in section 8(b)(ii) above. An emphasis should also be placed in health education for STD/HIV prevention, as well as measures to combat alcoholism and violence. ULBs should establish a network of community health workers/volunteers to facilitate this process through health promotion activity.

(iii) Private Sector Partnership

ULBs may consider establishing formal partnerships with private medical practitioners to undertake the delivery of curative services in slums. Such partnerships could provide greater outreach of services at low cost. Traditional systems of medicine may also be used where this expertise is available.

(iv) Health Insurance to Widen the Access to Curative Health Care

ULBs should encourage communities to participate in health insurance schemes in conjunction with the Saving and Credit society component of the Swarna Jayanti Rozgar Yojana (SJSRY) scheme and any other scheme for widening access to curative health care.

(b) Education

Attention and efforts should be focused on increasing the school enrollment at primary level, reducing school drop-out rates particularly for girls and supplementing formal school education with coaching assistance to assist slum children join the formal schooling system. The following specific measures will facilitate this process:

(i) Primary Education

ULBs should identify all informal settlements that are inadequately served with pre-school and primary schools facilities. Funds should then be made available under NSDP and other departmental programmes to address this problem on a priority basis with the most under serviced areas receiving priority assistance. Multi Purpose Community Centres (MPCC) may also be used for primary education where necessary.

(ii) Pre-Schools and Non-Formal Education

ULBs should actively promote pre-school/crèche facilities and non-formal education focusing on literacy and vocational training. Multi-Purpose Community Centres (MPCC) may be used for pre-schools/crèches facilities, non-formal education classes, adult education, recreational activities etc. It is to be emphasized that community management and control on the use of community centres is desirable to avoid misuse of this facility.

(iii) Community Management in Education

Mobilising the community and use of resource persons from within the community to supervise and monitor the educational activity would greatly enhance the delivery of this service. Contributions by way of space and building would build stakes of the community in the process of creating awareness demand for this service.

(iv) Education Incentive Scheme

Innovative incentive schemes may be established for those communities that show good performance in improving school attendance particularly in relation to the female child in both the formal and non-formal systems.

(v) Literacy

A strong emphasis should be placed on developing literacy skills especially for women and children. The ULB should ensure that all slum development schemes are properly integrated into state and national literacy initiatives and campaigns. Community halls and other public spaces may be used for holding literacy classes. NGOs wishing to participate in literacy schemes for slum dwellers should be given access to such halls and other facilities.

(vi) Day Crèche Facilities

ULBs should make provision for establishing day crèche facilities in all slums to enable women to participate more fully in the labour market. Community halls may be used for such purposes and parents may be encouraged to contribute to the cost of running and maintaining such facilities.

(c) Child Labour and Child Rights

ULBs should be active partners in the implementation of the international convention on child rights and should ensure that every child has access to a sufficient range of educational and vocational training. At the same time ULBs should discourage child labour through the implementation of penalties and fines and the withdrawal of licences for employers found to be suing child labour without making proper provision for education or training.

(d) Public Distribution System (PDS)

State Governments and ULBs may consider granting Community Development societies licences to operate Fair Price Shops where such societies have been set up and are seen to be running effectively. This will have the dual effect of strengthening the CDS structure and maximizing public satisfaction and welfare.

Municipal Services to be brought under Consumer Protection Act

It will be desirable to bring Municipal Services under the Consumer Protection Act to monitor quality and reliability of basic infrastructure services delivered at settlement level. This should be uniformly applied irrespective of tenure and land status of the settlement, with a specific mandate to monitor absolute levels of service coverage and differential levels of service availability throughout the ULB area. It is recommended that a special consumer panel be established in each municipality comprising members from different settlement categories (in proportion to their total number in the population) with authority to report to Council.

ECONOMIC EMPOWERMENT

(a) Financial Services for the Poor

The poor primarily require mechanisms that will encourage savings for small lump sums that can be used for a variety of consumption (including emergency) and production purposes. These mechanisms can also be used for credit purposes based on group (solidarity) lending principles, which involve incremental borrowing against social collateral (peer pressure). Such approaches have been seen to be far more successful ways of providing the poor with convenient access to credit on a sustainable basis (good internal discipline and low rates of default) than many of the subsidized schemes run by government which suffer from low levels of credit discipline, poor rates of repayment and high levels of leakage. Savings and credit groups can be further strengthened and supported through networking of such groups with each other to form a federated structure that may also access formal sources of credit.

UBLs should identify organizations with expertise in-group based savings and credit to promote financial service initiatives in slums wherever possible. The ULB may also wish to consider using such organizations and methodologies to implement government sponsored credit schemes such as SJSRY. To facilitate this process, it is recommended to create an apex body of saving and credit groups at city and state level. Possibility to enlarge the saving and credit services by contracting out to authorize financial intermediaries in the private sector shall also be explored.

The guiding principles for organizing savings and credit groups shall include: the group to identify its own members, help develop their own rules and regulations, encourage them to take decisions in terms of money to be saved, periodicity of savings, the purpose for which the money can be lent, amount to be lent, interest rates to be charged, repayment period etc. Any imposition or interference in this process will promote dependency and affect their confidence levels in terms of taking decisions and implementing the activities. The organizers of the community should also help people to acquire capacities in terms of maintenance of accounts, monitoring savings and loan programmes etc. to ensure that the discipline is established and sustained.

(b) Economic Support/Enterprise Development

There is a need for ULBs to support interventions designed to address livelihood needs of the urban poor. This will include:

- The provision of vocational training facilities;
- Implementation of savings and credit schemes for self-employment;
- Addressing constraints in the labour market;
- Providing improved access to raw materials and marketing support;

- Legal rights and redressal systems.

It would be desirable for the ULB to involve the private sector in such initiatives wherever possible.

For the people to participate, we have to create some mechanism through which they can participate. The

TABLE 3.1

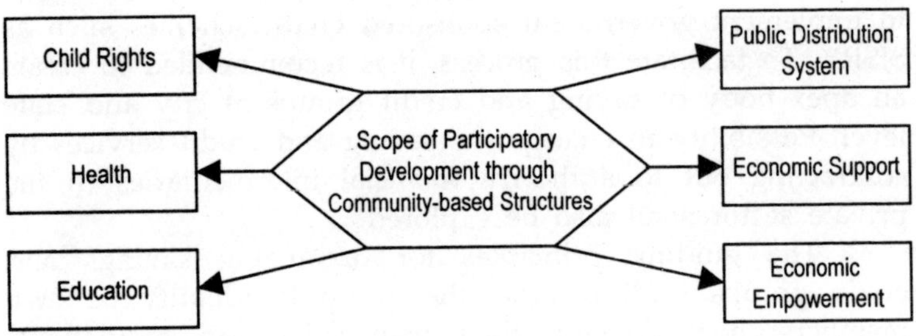

community-based organisations include Neighbourhood Groups (NHGs): Neighbourhood Committees (NHCs) and Community Development Society (CDSs).

I. Neighbourhood Group (NHG)

This is an informal association of women living in mohalla or basti or neighbourhood group of manageable size (preferably the 10 to 40 per cent represent urban poor or slum families), geographic contiguity and homogeneity should be the basis to carve out the boudarie of the NHGs. At least one woman resident among them who is willing to serve as a volunteer should be selected as a Resident Community Volunteer (RCV) through community consensus or election or any other democratic process. There should be a change or rotation (if need be) of such volunteers at periodical intervals. The responsibilities of RCVs include:

(i) to serve as a channel of information and communication among the families in the cluster;

(ii) to represent the views of the groups in the neighbourhood committees and community development societies and other forums;

(iii) to support planning, implementation and monitoring of activities at the neighbourhood level;
(iv) to foster and encourage participation in community improvement; and
(v) to motivate the community for being members of thrift and credit society; and to contribute to community development fund.

II. Neighbourhood Committees (NHCs)

A Neighbourhood Committee (NHC) is a more formal association of women from the above neighbourhood groups located in close proximity and as far as feasible within the same electoral ward. The Committee should consist of all the RCVs from the neighbourhood groups as executives (with voting right) of NHC as well as one female member (without voting rights) from each family, which falls under the jurisdiction of NHC concerned. There can also be provision for honorary membership without a voting right for Community Organisers (COs), representatives from other sectoral programmes in the community like ICDS supervisor, school teacher, ANM etc. the Convener/President of the NHC will be selected/elected by the executive members of the NHC. The Convener will ensure that the meetings are convened on regular basis. The NHC would be responsible for following activities:

Infrastructure and Function of Community Based Structures at Municipal

Level

(i) to identify local problems and priorities;
(ii) to provide suggestions for groups involvement in meeting community needs and goals (mini-plans);
(iii) to support local action with partnership of responsible agencies including community contracts;
(iv) to provide feedback to agencies of programme effectiveness and out-reach especially for children

and women;

(v) to develop community capacity through training in association with Cos, NGOs and other sectroal departments;

(vi) to develop community based thrift and credit system as well as neighbourhood development fund;

(vii) to facilitate the recovery of loans from the beneficiaries in time; and

(viii) to assist/carry out community surveys in accordance with the guidelines.

The NHC may be registered under the Societies Registration Act, or other appropriate acts if so desired. If registered, these NHC may also apply for grants-in-aid under various schemes.

III. Community Development Society (CDS)

The CDS is a formal association of all the neighbourhood development committees at the town level based on common goals and objectives. The CDS may consist of elected/selected representatives of NHCs as executive members (with voting right) as well as one female member from each family (without voting right) which falls under the jurisdiction of CDS; and other members with honorary membership (with no voting right) which may include community organisers, representatives of NGOs, sectroal department, leading citizens, elected representatives of the area and other resource persons. The Community Development Society (CDS) should be registered under the Societies Registration Act or other appropriate Acts to provide access to grant-in-aid under various schemes and for a wider Financial and credit base. The CDS would be responsible:

(i) to represent needs of all the communities, especially women and children;

(ii) liaise and link-up with agencies and departments to promote action in the community towards fulfilment of their needs;

(iii) to identify specific training and arrange for their organisation;

(iv) to facilitate community surveys to be carried out to identify the genuine beneficiaries for economic and shelter benefits;

(v) to prepare community plans and proposals, mobilising resources from the community, town or other sectoral departments;

(vi) to extend help to Bank in coordination with UPE Cell, for ensuring repayment of loans by the beneficiaries in time; and

(vii) to create small community assets in low income areas in consultation with town UPE Cell and Urban Local Body (ULB).[9]

Let us examine in detail the role, which the community structure can play in Urban Development:

Role of the Community Based Structures

(a) Promotes Participation of Beneficiaries

Voluntary organizations are nearer to the people and get better response from them in the implementation of programmes than official agencies and thus they are in a better position to render effective service. By and large, they have a better knack of communicating with the beneficiaries than members of official agencies. This of course, is a natural manifestation of the ancient civilization of India, which has attached the greatest importance to the participation of the people in decision-making. The mobilization of the energies and resources of the beneficiaries themselves is the key factor in increasing their welfare and self-reliance. People's participation through voluntary agencies in the promotion and economics of social welfare means involvement of the people in the process of social welfare voluntarily and willingly. Such participation cannot be forced. People's involvement can be assured through the participation of the beneficiaries in the decision-making, implementation, monitoring and evaluation of development programmes carried out by the voluntary agencies. This will lay the solid foundation in the prevention and promotion of services and the people would become self-reliant rather than depend on the help from the Municipal Government.

According to Dharma Vira:

> "Work of voluntary organization and citizen participation are two sides of the same coin. Citizens work in the organization but on there work depends the quality of the service the organization render. Voluntary Organizations provide a frame for citizen participation. Without effective participation, the organization would only be empty forums."[10]

Municipal staff is supposed to provide facilities for community based structures to function efficiently.

(b) Creating a Sense of Responsibility through Direct Involvement

Programme results are more successful and meaningful if the potential beneficiaries take part in their design and implementation through the forum of voluntary organizations. For example, if uncollected garbage draws files, or drains become clogged and overflow or if dirt pathways become ankle-deep mud sloughs in the rainy season, voluntary agencies will like to do something to remedy the situation from complaining to the Municipal Health Department to dredging canals and filing in muddy pathways themselves.

The more important role of voluntary agencies is, to stimulate active citizen participation in matters that concerns them and their community. How can this role be effectively played? Today, it is generally accepted that social and economic development cannot take place unless municipal staff breaks these forms of traditional intertia so that the masses can be imbued with confidence in their capacity to solve their own daily problems.

(c) Rectification of Planner's Mis-conception

It is very difficult for people to let their views be known individually while planners find it difficult to appreciate their needs. People's participation through voluntary agencies can rectify planning errors by making it possible for clients to point out to planners, policy-makers and administrators, what will work and what will not. Planning Agency created at the district local under 74th amendment of the constitution can really plan if the views of these community-based structures are taken into consideration. These views are based on reality and not theory. If things are left only to the specialists, they would ignore the genuine demands of the masses. The higher status experts thus set the framework of discussion and carry it through in categories meaningful to themselves but often incomprehensible to the ordinary, poor and lowly educated laymen.

(d) Greater Understanding and Positive Attitudes among the Beneficiaries (Formation of Public Opinion)

The involvement of the beneficiaries in the socio-economic development or city reconstruction is dependent to a great extent upon their enlightenment. This can take place when community based structures interpret and explain the issues and problems of Municipal administration to the public, e.g., cleanliness. The community based municipal structures are also trying to help by creating in the people an urge, an attitude to adopt new methods of development by arranging for the people services and opportunities to acquire new knowledge and techniques and by acting as a mediator between the people and the official machinery to interpret the problems and needs of the one to the other in order to develop better appreciation of each other.

(e) Effective Policy Formation Through Interpretation of Public Opinion

The community based municipal structures can present the real needs of development of the people to the various decision-making bodies to the Local self Govt. Department. Information is the policy-makers' raw material, forming the basis for his diagnosis, strengthening his projections and permitting him to evaluate the programmes, which have been planned. The degree to which a municipal planner will be able to plan in terms of needs will depend on the degree, to which he is able to obtain information about them, which is valid and reliable. The information supplied by voluntary agencies can be reliable as it is based on the outcome of their intimate contacts with the population.

(f) Flexibility and Experimentation

The Community Based Structures are autonomous in their functioning. They are not bound by well-defined laws and regulations, which are difficult to change. This gives them an opportunity to experiment with a given programme and adjust it according to the environmental conditions. The programme must develop environmental linkages in order to be of lasting value and benefit to the people. The autonomous character of the voluntary agencies provides them flexibility to adopt their programme according to the needs and aspirations of the people. We know that the best structure can come up only in a congenial soil. The problems of the people differ from city to city and hence, it is difficult to solve the problems for all the areas with the same solution. The voluntary organizations can experiment with different models in different areas and adopt and develop the best for the area for a given time dimension as the models of development are bound to change with the time dimension.

(g) Initiative and Leadership

Community Based Structures involve the people in the policy formulation and implementation of the programmes. This encourages the local potential leaders to develop as agents of socio-economic change. The people are not dependent on the initiative of the Municipal Government alone. They take the initiative and believe in self-help rather than help from outside.

(h) Channelise Human Resources

It is very difficult to provide all the social services to the people through the Municipal Government, as it is very costly. The voluntary agency can exploit the unused energies of the people for the development of the city. Energy of the people, if unused, cannot be preserved. This unused energy "like the unused vast water resources flowing down the Himalayas is not only wasted like those rivers, but also, like the river waters that take with them the top solid of the Himalayan region causing permanent losses in soil erosion, cause permanent damage to the human spirit and will in a community through dependence and frustration born out of ever-increasing level of abject poverty over the generations."[11]

(i) Advancing Social Legislation

In a welfare state, social welfare laws are as essential as security laws. These come under the purview of social legislation. It is the tool with which the social administrator is able to help the community from hazards. The social legislation need radical changes to cover all the people. Voluntary agencies can mobilize public opinion in support of such legislations. These agencies can prepare the people to act as a pressure group to motivate the Government to enact legislations for the welfare of the masses. A political system remains in equilibrium only if it channelises the demands of the people into policies and decisions beneficial to the people.

(j) Supplement the Efforts of Government

The problems of development are so vast and stupendous that it is difficult to solve these problems with the efforts of the Municipal Government machinery alone. There is a need to share this responsibility and the voluntary sectors, which possess immense potential, can take up this burden. During the last three decades, the municipal government have been trying to bring about socio-economic revolution but the progress has been halted because of the non-availability of needed resources. Thus, there is a need of a voluntary sector to supplement the efforts of the Government. The working group appointed by the Planning Commission remarked that the country's social and economic problems are so vast and multifarious that the Government's administrative machinery alone cannot tackle them. The establishment of a self-reliant society implies progressive curtailment of people's dependence on the Government. From time immemorial voluntary agencies in our country have played a significant part in promoting people's welfare.[12] Government has to assume the major responsibility, not only for developmental programmes, but also in providing leadership and resources for voluntary agencies to continue their work. This partnership or complimentary relationship now needed eventually be lessened to a point where it can be possible to have a demarcation of roles.

(k) Help in Efficient Programme Implementation

Community based municipal structures can help in the programme implementation, collaboration and co-ordination with other agencies. They can contribute to development in many ways through programme implementation. They can:[13]

(1) Provide assistance to develop and/or strengthen local NGO capabilities and activities with particular attention to local community development groups.
(2) Conduct reviews and assessment of existing development programmes and assist communities in the exercise of their own role in such reviews. A greater emphasis on evaluative techniques will render all new programmes more accountable to real community needs.
(3) Develop innovative ideas in the context of comprehensive human development.
(4) Ensure that their existing programmes and new initiatives promote full participation by individuals and communities in the planning, implementation and control of these programmes.
(5) Expand their training efforts to respond to the needs of development eg., training of health workers, supervisors, administrators, planners and various agricultural and development workers.
(6) Extend their efforts to develop locally sustainable and appropriate technologies and use of resources, with particular attention to energy, water, agriculture, sanitation and medical care.
(7) Contribute to the creation of new and effective methods of health education, which enable both individuals and communities to assume greater responsibility for their own health.
(8) Recognize the essential roles of women in health

promotion and in the full range of community development concerns.

They can further extend their capacity to work with poor, disadvantaged and remote populations enabling them to break the cycle of deprivation, and in this way contribute to the search for greater social justice."[14]

Thus NHG, NHC and CDS can play an important role in the development of Basties which have become a scar to the fair name of a city as well as make the lives of the people living in these Basties healthier happier and prosperous Basties can become an integral part of the city and not isolated structures.

CONCLUSION

Though slum improvement is the responsibility of Union, State and Local Governments, but the main thrust lies on the initiative, involvement and participation by slum dwellers.

Notes and References

1. William A. Robson D.E. Regan, (ed.), Great Cities of the World, Their Government, Politics and Planning, Volume I, p. 62.
2. Arne F. Leemans in his Article on "Amsterdam" in *Ibid.*
3. Fouad D. Alided - Tawal in his Article on "Cairo" in *Ibid.*, p. 162.
4. Ali Ashraf and Hestile Green in their articles on Calcutta, in *Ibid.*, pp. 292-293.
5. Alihijit Datta and J.N. Khosla in their article on "Delhi" in *Ibid.*, p. 435.
6. Government of India, Planning Commission, Tenth Five Year Plan (2002-2007), Volume II, Sectoral Policies and Programmes, p. 611.
7. *Ibid.*, p. 612.
8. *Ibid.*, p. 631.
9. Swarn Jayanti Shahari Rozgar Yojana, (SJSRY) Guidelines, pp. 16-17.
10. Dharam Vira, "Citizen Participation" in Encyclopaedia of Social Work, Vol. I, p. 102.
11. Malhotra, R.C., *op. cit.*, p. 11.
12. GOI, Planning Commission, Report of the Working Group on Block Level Planning, 1978, pp. 139-140.
13. World Federation of Public Health Associations, *op. cit.*, pp. 45-46.
14. Social Welfare Administration, Vol. 2.

4

Capacity Building: Education and Training to Resident Community Volunteers

INTRODUCTION

The success of participatory development depends upon the enthusiasm, confidence, interest and motivation among the women living in Bastis especially those who have been identified and designated as Resident Community Volunteers. They are illiterate women living in extreme poverty and adverse circumstances. They have not been exposed to newer ways of life. We expect them to play a major role in community development with the support of community organizers, Assistant Project Officers and SUDA. How can they be equipped to perform this new role? The answer is education and training to RCVS, which can change their vision, outlook and perception. We now discuss the important areas, which can serve as contents of education and training.

Since inception, GOI has invested huge amounts to improve the lives of urban people through various schemes enumerated earlier. However the most important component is education and training of community volunteers which can remove inertia and make the employees of urban local bodies and the beneficiaries to accelerate the process of socio-economic development. Education is basic tool for the development of consciousness and reconstitution of Society.

Dr. S. Ignacimuthu, S.J., Vice Chancellor, Bharathiar University, said:

> "It is only through education we can address the challenges of poverty, ignorance and under-development. It is education that will help us to harness the great human potential which is our biggest asset, and it is education which is the key to providing for all our people the health and prosperity which is the key to providing for all our people the health and prosperity which is their right."

Education is one of the most important factors in achieving the development goals of the Municipal services. It is the key to the municipal development. It is an investment in the human resources. If the fruits of education have to reach the common man, it must be adequately and properly administered.

TRAINING TO COMMUNITY VOLUNTEERS (RCV)

Community Volunteers possess immense potential energy. This can be translated into kinetic energy provided this is channelized through practical training. Training is essential to make the Volunteers capable, active and motivated. What should be the contests of such training programmers? Let us discuss the important aspects that need to be covered in these training programmes. More that two dozen training programmes were organized at various places in the state to suit the convenience of RCV.

1. Creating Confidence among Resident Community Volunteers

Training should ensure that the women become confident and sure of their potentialities. Training can help them in taking their own decisions concerning their lives. Confidence, once created, will generate chain reactions in ushering socio-economic development of the area. The idea that they are as important as other citizens of the city must be ingrained in their minds so that their inferiority complex is removed. All this has to be done with love, affection, sincerity and devotion on the part of trainers and community organizers.

2. Making them Understand the Importance or Cleanliness of Home and the Environment

Cleanliness is next to godliness. They must be made aware about small things like clean water, cleanliness of surroundings, proper drainage etc. as most of the diseases spread through unclean environment. To get pure water and pure air, environment must be clean.

3. Making Volunteers understand Changing Status of Women and Need to Harness Potential Female Energy for National Development

"That society would be highly developed and prosperous where women have their rightful place" expounds Manu.

The woman is the pivot around which the family, the society and humanity itself revolves. It is well said that the hands that rock the cradle rule the world. Women play a significant role in the development of their offspring. Truly if man is educated, one person is educated but if the woman is educated, the whole family is educated.

Much that has been granted to women by law is yet to be within the reach of them all, in reality. Continual large scale effort is needed to liquidate the limitations still suffered by women to work shoulder to shoulder for improving the standard of living of the Indian masses so that opportunities for living a richer and fuller life would be available to both women and men.[1]

Today, technological advancements and, in general, developments in every sphere and the race against time have compelled women to come out of the confines of the house and contribute more to the stream of life. It is a pity that a large majority of Indian women are still steeped in ignorance and have not been able to break themselves away from the clutches of old rituals, traditions and beliefs. Only a microscopic minority of womenfolk has been able to utilize the rights enshrined in the Constitution. The time has come for women to march side by side with men. To shoulder this new responsibility effectively, women have to be better equipped and qualified.

National development depends a great deal on the welfare of women who are the real architects of a nation. The programme for women welfare aims at raising the economic and social status of women so that they can play an important role in building a strong and prosperous nation.

The reason for poverty and misery in the developing countries is not essentially the lack of potentialities or resources, whether human or material but under-utilization of these resources. Today, developing countries are not utilizing more than 15 pre cent of the potential capacity of this manpower.[2] A plausible remedy to increase the GNP and improve the standard of living, it appears, is the maximum utilization of more than 51 per cent of the world population, that is, women. This calls for an active participation of women on a bigger scale in the task of development, national reconstruction and social change. As Helvi Sipila, a Finnish lawyer, who was the UN's Secretary-General for the International women's Year says:

> "We cannot hope to solve the increasing international problems of economic and social development, and improve the quality of human life while leaving aside half the resources of humanity."[3]

There is a need to harness stagnant and un-exploited potential female energy. The Economic and social survey of Asia and the Pacific, also stresses the same view.

> "The wastage of human resources that results from the exclusion of women from the development forces is something that developing countries can ill-afford. This wastage can take the form of the use of a large part of women's time in carrying out domestic tasks amenable to increased efficiency through some investment."[4]

We should not think that we can conceive of women development independently of the socioeconomic development of the country. Women development could contribute to the development and modernization of the world.

A similar message was conveyed by the UNESCO that women can play an important part in development. They represent the means through which the changes in attitudes and behaviour necessary for adaptation to the modern world can be achieved. Their responsibility for bringing up new generations means that they must also attend to the education of children and supervise their scholastic progress and critical faculty. As home managers, they have the task of improving the conditions of the family life while as household administrators, they must balance the financial budget. A UN report also support this view:

> "The exclusion of women from many aspects of the development process also has important indirect effects. First, there is the effect on the nature of their influence on the education and socialization of their children, because by and large, women will pass on their own experience and attitudes. Secondly, there is the indirect effect on population growth. This is an extremely complex subject. Though it is not easy to isolate the factors affecting fertility, many of the relevant factors can be combined under the heading of exposure of women to modernization."[5]

During the last three decades, a number of movements began to 'raise the consciousness' of women with regard to their inferior status and to seek ways of improving it. These movements were born and nurtured wherever women had access to national, regional and global activities. The leaders of these movements were becoming more aware of the realities of the situation, they're own and that of other women. Women have a clear perception that participation in socio-economic development of their country was not only their right but much of their responsibility. Helvi Sipila, UN Assistant secretary-general for Social development and

Humanitarian Affairs, has rightly said that: "Lack of full appreciation of the situation of women and of its vital importance to society as a whole had prevented most governments and inter-governmental organizations, including those in the United Nations System, from giving any priority to the various international resolutions adopted by the UN and its agencies in order to improve the status of women and integrate them in to the life of society. Only a limited number of non-governmental organizations, mostly women's organizations, dealt with these issues in "splendid isolation" amongst themselves, especially on the national level, where joint efforts alone could strengthen their position as a pressure group."[6]

The 27th UN General Assembly, acting on the initiative of number of women's organizations, proclaimed 1975 as "International Year for Women" as there was a lot of discrimination against women. This discrimination was responsible for oppression of women:

> "Poverty, illiteracy, confinement to the house, under nutrition and superstition tend not only to reinforce but also to perpetuate a pattern of idleness and low efficiency in all activities including agriculture and to inhibit the full utilization of women as human resources for national development."[7]

The theme of the IWY "Equality, Development and peace" was considered to be an appropriate reflection of the principles contained in the Geneva Convention, the league of Nations and the UN Charter,[8] and the subsequent resolution of the United Nations and its Specialized Agencies. As a result of the approval of this theme, the General Assembly elaborated it further and mentioned in concrete forms its objectives as:

(a) to promote equality between men and women;
(b) to ensure the full integration of women in the total development effort, especially by emphasising women's responsibility and important role in economic, social and cultural development

at the National, Regional and International level, particularly during the Second Development Decade; and

(c) to recognize the importance of women's increasing contribution to the development of friendly relations and cooperation among states to the strengthening of world peace.[9]

IMPROVING EDUCATION STATUS OF WOMEN THROUGH ADULT EDUCATION AND FUNCTIONAL LITERACY

Prof. Amritya Sen states:

"An illiterate person is that much less equipped to defend herself in court, to obtain bank loan, to enforce her inheritance right, to take advantage of new technology, to compete for securing employment, to get on the right bus, to take part in political activity, to participate successfully in the modern economy and society."

All women reforms will remain a dream unless women are themselves enlightened. Education is the key factor in elevating the status of women. It equips them to contribute in different fields more meaningfully. Many of the national programmes like Family Planning, Grow More Food, Cottage Industries are not a great success because of lack of creative participation of the people and especially the women.[10]

The National Plan of Action for Women mentioned the following causes responsible for the low literacy among women in India:

(a) General indifference to education of girls.
(b) Social resistance arising out of fears and misconceptions that education might alienate girls form traditions and social values and lead to maladjustment's, conflicts and non-conformism.
(c) Early marriage and social inhibition against girls pursing education after marriage.
(d) Prevalence of child labour among girls belonging

to weaker sections and the hard domestic chores which some of the unmarried girls especially from middle and lower middle class families are required to perform.

(e) The prevailing notion that the sole occupation of women is to bear children, look after her husband and children, and thus be restricted to domestic work.

(f) Discrimination effected by employers against women labour in both organized and unorganized sectors in matters of recruitment, training and promotion.

(g) Many girls and their parents find that the school curriculum does not conform adequately to their needs and interests.

(h) Unsuitable and inflexible school timings and inadequate facilities for girls in schools, particularly in the co-educational schools."[11]

Education is the most potent factor for changing women's position in society. We must correct the imbalances by encouraging the education of girls. We can use the adult education or non-formal education system. What can be the future of a country where general illiteracy, especially among women, is very high? Besides, the women have also to handle the new generation i.e. the child who is the future hope.

All this would remain a dream unless women are themselves enlightened. Education is the key factor in elevating the status of women. It equips them to contribute in different fields more meaningfully. Dr. (Mrs.) P.K. Devi, Professor of Gyneacology, in PGI, Chandigarh, has rightly stated on the basis of her critical examination among the various States of the Indian Union, that "Literacy, especially of women seems to be a significant factor in differences in the mortality and morbidity rates between various Indian states and infant mortality rates coincide with a very low female literacy rate."[12]

It may be concluded that women education can help in nation building. Napoleon once said,

"Give me good mothers, I will give you a good nation."

Illiteracy is a great obstruction in the path of development and education is the backbone of democracy. The Director General of UNESCO has described illiteracy as "the most monstrous of all the many instances of wasted human potential which still at the present time keeps more than one third of the human race in a sate of hopelessness-below the level of modern civilisation." Therefore, in order to translate the essence of the Preamble and the Directive Principles of the State Policy enshrined in the Constitution in India in to practical life, it is imperative for us to increase the literacy rate in general and of women in particular.[13]

IMPROVING OPPORTUNITIES FOR ORGANIZED AND UNORGANIZED EMPLOYMENT

Planners are generally agreed that one of the most important means of improving the status of women is to secure for them a fair share of employment opportunities.[14] Further, it is postulated that a decline in women's employment adversely affects trends in fertility, mortality and nutrition.[15]

(a) Limited overall opportunities available for wage employment.
(b) Attitudes to wage employment and working women, whether by women themselves, by men or society at large.
(c) Prejudices of employees in terms of women's employment.
(d) Inadequate education/training opportunities for women and attitudes to such educational training.
(e) Lack of easily available information and guidance on carrier choice, i.e., vocational counselling.

EDUCATION TO VOLUNTEERS ABOUT THE AVAILABILITY OF HEALTH SERVICES IN THEIR AREA

Health facilities are undoubtedly inadequate especially in Bastis of a city. The women services have four components-care of general medical problems; care of gynecological problems; obstetric care and family problems; obstetric care and family planning. The purpose is to provide planned maternal and child health services to ensure that expectant and nursing mothers maintain good health, have a normal delivery and bear healthy children. It is a service planned for the promotion and restoration of health of mothers and children and provision of safe confinement. Women volunteers may be educated about the Govt. sponsored health services like sub-centre. Subsidiary Health Centre and Primary Health Centre. They may be introduced to Health Personnel working in these institutions so that convergence with health services can be ensured.

EDUCATION ABOUT NUTRITION AND NUTRITIONAL SERVICES

The most serious problem afflicting women is lack of adequate nutrition. Girls and Women generally get the leftovers because of the social customs, poverty and the poor social status. A pleasant and healthy diet, not necessarily an expensive one is one of the most satisfying and stimulating activities of family life. It contributes to the physical, the mental and social well being of the family.

We must educate volunteers that nature abounds in good nutritious food within reach of the economically under privileged families. A balanced diet does not mean an expensive diet. With proper education, families with limited financial resources can take better care of their nutritional needs. It is, therefore, essential for the health department of the municipalities and voluntary organizations to impart this type of education as this can go a long way in promoting the health and well being of family members. Health institutions do not provide, at present, any special nutritional services. There is a need to plan well equipped and staffed nutrition clinics attached to all hospitals and PHCs. There may be arrangements to educate the women about the nutritive value of locally available foods and also teach methods of cooking that would retain food value. The properties of medical herbs and medicines and traditional cures can be analyzed and popularized among mothers.[16] This is more important in Punjab as women are mal-nourished inspite of plenty of hour. All these must be told during training and special lectures.

EDUCATION ABOUT PLANNING ADEQUATE FAMILY WELFARE PROGRAMMES

Poor women are burdened with large number of children resulting into poor health of mothers and children. They may be educated and encouraged to adopt family planning. In Bastis women start their reproductive life when they are barely out of adolescence and may have four to five children by the time they are thirty. This adversely affects their health and well being.

Women in the rural and urban areas have hardly any say in family planning. It is men who decide matters, but among the educated women, some mutual understanding is evident. The education of women, population changes and overall development is closely interrelated. Women have a crucial role to play in all these areas still uncovered. A study of the inter relationship of the status of women and family planning was conducted in accordance with the Economic and Social Council Resolution.[17] The report affirmed:

(a) The right to decide freely and responsibly on the number and spacing of their children is a fundamental right of individuals which facilitates the exercise of other human rights especially by women;

(b) Adequate information, education and services enabling individuals to exercise this right are essential pre-requisites for the promotion of the status of women, and for ensuring their complete integration in social and economic development at all levels;

(c) Family planning which should constitute an integrated and essential part of development plan and programmes; in countries suffering from over population can only succeed in concert with other measures which also improve the status of women.

The establishment of a close doctor patient relationship is an absolutely essential requirement for the success of the programme, careful follow up by doctors of vasectomy and tubectomy cases is as necessary as the operation itself, for the physchological rehabilitation of the patient, as well as for the assurance of potential acceptors.[18]

IMPARTING EDUCATION FOR FAMILY HEALTH

Healthy families make healthy people. The family is the primary unit of health care, a front line in the sequence of education, prevention, diagnosis, treatment and rehabilitation of its constituents. "Health begins at Home" was the theme chosen for World Health Day (1973) on 25th Anniversary of WHO in recognition of the important role of the family in promoting and protecting the health of its members. Women occupy an important place in shaping the lives of its family members. The mothers are still the best teachers about life and health. The education imparted by her remains with children as long as they live. Government should provide health education to women as notions of health and hygiene given at home to children would help them to be good citizens. Women if properly educated can really help in the socio-economic development of the country. This would release the potential energy of the women for channeling the welfare of the family and ultimately national development.

TRAINING WOMEN IN THE ART AND SCIENCE OF PARTICIPATION IN THERE OWN WELFARE

Women should themselves exert pressure to get the due benefits for their welfare. They should unite to from voluntary organizations to help themselves and ultimately the nation. It was rightly stated in the National Plan of Action for women that:

> "Women voluntary organizations are best suited for motivation in the field of health, family planning and nutrition. There is therefore, every need for creating a conducive climate, so that they can render the needed services effectively."[19]

In this implementation process, women themselves will have to be the most forceful agents for change and active participants in the development effort, wherever they have the opportunity to play a dynamic role. The contemporary social situation of women in India should not be frustrating and disheartening but should be rather challenging and it is the men and women of India, particularly the women who have to face the challenge. The women in the field have demonstrated that they are as capable and efficient as men in carrying out various kinds of work are and have even much more endurance for hardships than is commonly believed. All of us, who are associated with the development of the country in any capacity, must renew our dedication to the cause of women, which would lead to national development.

TRAINING FOR CHILD DEVELOPMENT

Children are our future and our most precious resources. The quality of tomorrow's world and perhaps even it is the well being, safety and the physical and intellectual development of children will determine survival today. To predict the future of a nation, it has been remarked, one need not consult the stars; it can more easily and plainly be read in the faces of its children. Children are the mirrors of a nation. Abraham Lincoln nicely explained the role of the child, when he said:

> "A child is a person who is going to carry on what you have started. He is going to sit where you are sitting, and when you are gone attend to those things

which you think are important. You may adopt all the policies you please, but how they are carried out depends on him. He will assume control of your cities, states, and nations. He is going to move in and take over your Churches, Schools, Universities and Corporations. All your books are going to be judged, praised or condemned by him. The fate of humanity is in his hands."

The UN General Assembly in the Resolution comprising the Second Development Decade has stated:

"Today youth, everywhere is in ferment. The 1970's must mark a step forward in securing the well being and happiness not only of the present generation but also of the generations to come."[20]

One of the specific objectives of the Second Development Decade is that "the well-being of children shall be fostered."[21] Dr. P.C. Chunder, former Minister of Education and Social Welfare, Government of India in his Foreword to the National Plan of Action for International Year of the Child," 1979 has rightly said that,

"A Nation's children are its supremely important asset and the nation's future lies in their proper development... An investment in children is indeed an investment in the Nation's future. A healthy and educated child of today is the active and intelligent citizen of tomorrow."[22]

To quote C. Subraminam, the former Finance Minister in the Government of India:

"Giving high priority to children's welfare means singling out a target group which is intermingled with the rest of the population right down to the level of individual families. Therefore, it requires building up an organization and an administrative setup that goes all the way from international agencies to each village and town of less developed countries."[23]

To quote Mahatma Gandhi:

"If we are to reach real peace in this world and if we are to carry on a real war against war, we shall have to begin with children; and if they will grow up in their natural innocence we won't have to struggle, we won't have to pass fruitless ideal resolutions, but we shall go from love to love and peace to peace."

Effective national policies and plans regarding children can make a decisive contribution to all other long term development activities and particularly to the success of the programmes aimed at rising the quality of life of lower income groups and at building national capacities and self-reliance.

TRAINING IN TAKING COLLECTIVE DECISIONS ON THEIR OWN WELFARE

The ultimate success of participatory development rests upon their meeting together and plans for collective welfare.

Education and capacity building constitute the key to development, besides being the basic tools for empowering women. The education for improving the status of women is warranted at two levels—one of the citizens in general, and the other specifically targeting poor and disadvantaged women. The education of the general public should stress on improving gender sensitivity, creating equal opportunities and mitigating superstitions and social evils. Education and training specifically for the women should encompass vital inputs for awareness generation, enhancing knowledge base, skill levels and earning power, developing communication ability, improving enterprise skill and self portrayal as well as building confidence besides fostering a team-work approach for participatory decision making.

The main aim of the programmes should be to address the comprehensive upliftment in terms of their economic and social necessities, to ensure their absorption in the city

CHART 4.1

Capacity Building of Resident Community Volunteers

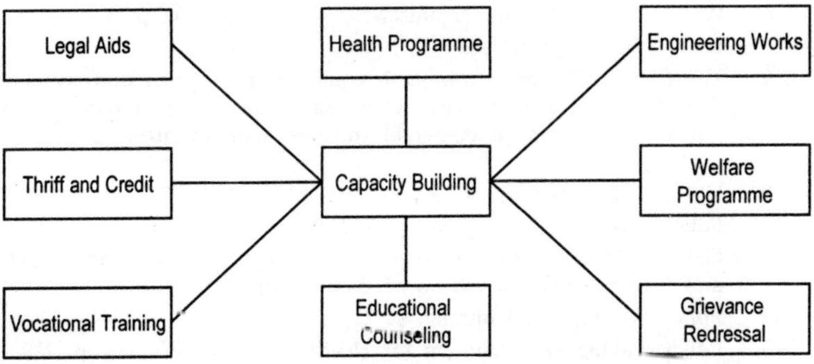

system, both as a participant and partner in its governance.

Once these volunteers shed their, inertia, the process of development would be very fast and the life of the city would become better and peaceful. Many problems facing city today i.e. law and order, unemployment prostitution, environment pollution would disappear. A personal observation of RCVS training at Patiala revealed that REVS are enthusiastic and keen to develop their Bastis they were hopeful of the future. They are thankful to SUDA for having given importance to them to do something for their own area.

CONCLUSION

Resident Community Volunteers are the kingpins in the process of participatory development. Therefore, there is a need to train them in the art and science of participation, so that they can help in the improvement of slum life.

NOTES AND REFERENCES

1. Raksha Sen : "Status of Women" Encycolpaedia of Social Work in India. Vol. II, p. 374.
2. UNDP; 12th Session of the UNDP-Governing Council, 7-23, June 1971, pp. 112-114.

3. The Tribune, Chandigarh, June 22, 1975.
4. UN : ESCAP : Economics and Social Survey of Asia and the Pacific, 1976, Bangkok, 1976, p. 56.
5. *Ibid.*
6. WHO : World Health Organisation, Aug-Sept., 1976, p. 3.
7. UN : E/CN, 6/583/. Add. 2, p. 14.
8. The Charter Preamble sets forth equal rights of 'men and women' and Art. I of the charter, "Universal respect and observance of human rights and fundamental freedom without distinction as to sex".
9. UN : 627TH Meeting of General Assembly—31.1.1974.
10. Policy-making and Planning, p. 219
11. Govt. of India: (Deptt. of Social Welfare) Blueprint of Action Points and National Plan of Action of Women, pp. 1-2.
12. Policy-making and Planning, p. 228.
13. Policy-making and Planning for Health Needs of Women, p. 229.
14. Sixth Five Year Plan, *op. cit.*, p. 148.
15. Ashok Mitra, Literacy and Employment (Bombay, Indian Council of Social Science Research Programme of Women's Studies, Allied Publishers Pvt. Ltd., p. 21.
16. Policy-making and Planning for the Health Needs of Women, p. 230.
17. UN : E/CN . 6/575 and Add 13 of ECOSOC: 16, 1326 (XLIV)
18. Policy-making and Planning for the Health Needs of Women.
19. National Plan of Action for Women, p. 71.
20. UN General Assembly, Second Development Decade, Report of the Second Committee (Part I) A/8/24.
21. Second Development Decades Resolution 2626 (XXV), para 18.
22. Govt. of India: Ministry of Education and Social Welfare, Department of Social Welfare: National Plan of Action for International Year of the Child (1979), New Delhi, September 1978.
23. Subramanian, C., "A World Charter for Children", The Hindu, 28 September, 1978.

5

Training to Municipal Officers, Assistant Project Officers and Community Organisers in the Art and Science of Slum Development

One of the key factors in the effort of the government to accomplish its developmental goals is to enhance its administrative capability for development at all levels of an administrative hierarchy, which is very much a part of the development process. Our experience during the last three decades has demonstrated that the development plans have not been satisfactorily implemented because of inadequate administrative performance. The reasons for the low level of administrative performance include: organizational defects, lack of coordination, complex and cumbersome administrative and financial procedures. These defects and deficiencies need to be corrected in order to bring about a sharp reduction in the administrative obstacles to development and to bridge the gap between aspirations and performance. Simultaneously, training them in modern concepts and techniques of administration and management can raise the level of competence of public service personnel directly involved in the execution of projects and implementation of development plans. This category of personnel at the senior or intermediate levels, comprising both technocrats and generalists, is constantly called upon to discharge increasingly heavy administrative and managerial responsibilities. In order to equip such personnel with the required expertise, skill, methodology and aptitude, there is a definite need to train them.

All agree that right training of the civil service is the first priority for developing countries. Training is: (a) an action process, (b) by which capabilities of the personnel can be improved, (c) to meet the organizational needs in terms of their knowledge, skills, and attitudes required in performing organizational tasks and functions, (d) within relatively short period of time.

Training is the well-articulated effort to promote competence in the public service by imparting professional knowledge, by broadening of vision and adoption of correct patterns of behaviour among the employees with regard to their existing functional responsibilities. It also enables the employees to equip themselves for senior administrative positions in future:

OBJECTIVES OF TRAINING

The objective of the training is to provide an individual with the knowledge of the environmental or ecology under which he is to function; the knowledge of administrative management to achieve optimum performance and cultivation of necessary attitudes.

(a) Environmental or Ecological Understanding

An employee must understand the legal framework under which he is to operate. He must be provided with the basic knowledge of social sciences to understand the intricacies of social environment. With the knowledge of social sciences he can react with the environment favourably. A.R. Tyagi, has justified it from three different points:

(i) Administration is a human process largely depending upon first hand experience drawn from the actual administrative situation in all its facets and on weighing each problem from every angle.

(ii) The role of public servant in a welfare state is that of a social scientist in action. In order to be able to act properly and effectively, he must have scientific acumen, which he can develop only by systematic and sustained education in theory and practice of social science.

(iii) The need for a basic training in the fundamentals of social science becomes all the more necessary in the context of our public recruitment being based on lower age limit; which limits the entry of advanced research students to the public service.[1]

(b) Improving Administrative Capability

There is a great need to enhance the administrative capability of public services so that they can achieve the objectives of the government in the shortest possible time. Administrative capability is an important means of converting or processing programme inputs into outputs such as goods and services. Kantz says: "Administrative capability for development involves the ability to mobilize, allocate and combine the actions that are technically needed to achieve development objectives."[2] It is felt that experimentation is costly and slow process. As such, we need to learn from the experience of others and use their results to help achieve our goals. In this context, Ernest Dale and L.C. Michelon observe that, "Today's manager lives in a world of rapid change, yet the rate of change is likely to increase in the years ahead. Unless he can keep up with this change, he is likely to find himself obsolete-perhaps un-promotable or even un-employable."[3]

(c) Cultivating Genuine Attitudes

Administration is manned by and meant for human beings. Administration is the art of conducting human affairs. Training must also aim to cultivate a new attitude and behaviour in human personality. In the public services, this is more important than the other two objectives. Marshall suggests the development of the following ingredients to promote right and rational attitudes.[4]

(i) development of rational thinking,
(ii) development of objective thinking,
(iii) development of social understanding,
(iv) development of aesthetic responsiveness,
(v) development of practical abilities, and
(vi) development and placement of memory in action.

TRAINING CONTENTS

The training courses generally include the following aspects:

(a) Job Aspects

Knowledge of the job, that has to be supervised, planning procedures, work analysis, methods of work, organization and co-ordination and cost analysis of the services.

Understanding the Importance of Environment

A Good Environment is the key to health and development. Environment has been defined by Webster's New Collegiate Dictionary as "the aggregate of all the external conditions and influences affecting the life and development of an organism".

Shri T.N. Chaturvedi in his Editorial to JPA, July-Sept. 1989 (Special Number on Environment and Administration) rightly sees the intimate relationship between human beings and nature since times immemorial. To quote:

> "Man, since his origin, has lived in harmony with Nature through the ages, holding Nature in awe and reverence. The Vedas, folklore and scriptures of different religions, faiths and beliefs also speak of the need for harmony with the universe, which is the habitat not only of man but also of all animals, birds, insects, plants and vegetation. The mutually supportive role of arriving things is often mentioned as a crucial factor for a balanced social and harmonious existence. The ecological balance is inherent in the very process of creation. Everywhere, the seers, poets and thinkers,

though the ages, have referred to the need for living in harmony with environment. In fact, the Taitariyupanishad looks at the relationship between man and his environment in its totality and stresses complete harmony and interdependence between them in order to attain real prosperity."

Dr. Hiroshi Nakjima, Director-General of World Health Organization, sounded a warning alarm about degradation of this planet in his Article "A Wounded planet". He rightly visualizes that it is now increasingly evident that more and more diseases stem from the degradation caused by man to his own environment. The potential harmful effects of industrial development on our global ecosystem are now better known. Ozone layer depletion, acid rain, climate change, chemical pollution is some examples of the man-made wounds to our planet.[5]

We are at a turning point; warnings of the damage to our health and quality of life are growing louder. An increasing number of people are acting to stop the degradation of our environment. Lt. Gen. J.F.R. Jacob, PVSM (Retd.) Governor, Punjab in his message "Fifty years of Indian Republic" in the Daily Tribune (26th January 2000), remarked that with our rising population the civil services and environment, especially in the urban areas, are under great stress and strain. The degradation of our environment has to be arrested immediately otherwise it would have long-term impact on the quality of life of future generations. We should also take this opportunity to educate our children regarding the importance of the preservation of our environment. Dr. Wilfried Kreisel also elaborates the aspects of environment, which affect health of mankind.[6]

How can we make environmental health a more potent force to serve people faced with growing threats to their health? How can our improving environmental health technology be better used to foster positive health? I know of no country developing or industrialized in which this issue is not urgent and important. I know of many countries in which it is critical.

The remarkably wide range of environmental concerns

includes the international problems of acid rain, the greenhouse effect, and depletion of the planet's ozone layer. It includes national concerns with medical wastes disposal, radioactive and toxic wastes control, transportation accidents, health aspects of urbanization and traffic, occupational health and safety, and air and water pollution. It also includes local concerns over inadequate water supplies and sanitation facilities, water quality, clean air, solid wastes management, and finding a balance between the economic incentives of development and a decent quality of life. In the report on Our Common Future, the World Commission on Environment and Development (sometimes called the Brundtland Commission) pointed out that the situation is getting increasingly critical.

Priority need to be accorded by the urban local bodies to promote environmental education create environmental awareness among various age-groups and to disseminate information through Environmental Information System (ENVIS) network to all concerned. Special emphasis is given to non-formal environmental education through seminars/ symposia/workshops, training programmes, Eco-camps, audio-visual shows, etc.

Over the years, together with a spreading of environment consciousness, there has been a change in the traditionally-held perception that there is a trade-off between environmental quality and economic growth as people have come to believe that the two are necessarily complementary. The current focus on environment is not new environmental considerations have been an integral part of the Indian culture. The need for conservation and sustainable use of natural resources has been expressed in Indian scriptures, more than three thousand years old and is reflected in the constitutional, legislative and policy framework as also in the international commitments of the country.[7]

AWARENESS OF POPULATION EXPLOSION (See Table 5.1)

The problem of growing population has reached such menacing proportions that it has become a real threat to the socio-economic stability of the country. The excessive growth

TABLE 5.1

Decadal Variations in Population Growth in India, 1901-2001

*Census Year**	*Total population in million*	*Average annual exponential growth rate*	*Progressive growth rate over 1901 in per cent*
1901	238.4	—	—
1911	252.1	0.56	5.8
1921	251.3	-0.03	5.4
1931	279.0	1.04	17.0
1941	318.7	1.33	33.7
1951	361.1	1.25	51.5
1961	439.2	1.96	84.3
1971	548.2	2.20	129.9
1981	683.3	2.22	186.6
1991	846.3	2.14	255.0
2001	1027.0	1.93	330.8

* Including Assam and Jammu and Kashmir. The 1981 Census was not held in Assam and the 1991 Census was not held in Jammu and Kashmir due to disturbances. The 1981 and 1991 census data include estimated figures for these two states.

Sources: Census of India 1971, General Population Tables, Series 1, India, part II-A (i), pp. 33,50, 536-37; Census of India 1991, final Population Totals: Brief Analysis of Primary Census Abstract, Series, 1, India, Part 2 of 1992, p.86; Census of India 2001, Provisional Population totals, series 1, India, Paper 1 of 2001, p. 34.

in population does not affect the stability of the national economy alone, it disturbs the stability of the entire body politic. It poses a colossal threat to our social structure. In our fight against poverty, disease, hunger malnutrition and unemployment, checking the rapid growth of population is as important as raising production in the farms and factories and provision of social services. Population control is one of the chief issues, which the country has to resolve and accord top priority in its march towards social and economic development. The programme of family planning is of vital importance for our country. It is a positive and constructive approach to the betterment of the quality of life of the community. Thus, it is evident that the key to India's economic future based on social justice lies in the immediate and effective implementation of a nation wide population programme.

According to the provisional results of the 2001 census, India's population stood at 1,027 million on March 1, 2001, comprising 531 million males and 496 million females. From 361 million at the time of Independence, the population reached one billion in 2001, registering an increase of nearly three times. All this had happened when the country is not in a position to guarantee adequate nutrition, health care and education to the burgeoning population. At the same time, it is also true that all this has happened because of mass poverty in the country. Indifferent governance is also partly responsible for the current demographic and health scenario. Every year about 18 million people were added to India's population during 1991-2001 as against 16 million annually during 1981-91 (see Chart 5.1). In other words, each year India's population increases by the equivalents of the number of inhabitants of Ghana, Australia, Mozambique or Saudi Arabia.[8]

The objectives of population should be to enable the people to understand that family size is controllable, that population limitation can facilitate the development of a higher equality of life in a nation and that a small size family can contribute to the quality of living for the individual family. It should also enable the people to appreciate the fact that for preserving the health and welfare of members of the family, to ensure the economic stability of the family and to assure good prospects for the younger generation, that the Indian families of today and tomorrow should be small and compact.

The Seminar giving a comprehensive definition of population education emphasized knowledge about the quantity and quality of population and the need to control them for happy human existence. Population education has been regarded as a strategy for human resource development. It aims at developing desired awareness, values and attitudes both for quality and quantity of population. It must enable students to make rational decisions on population matters for themselves and for others by acquiring knowledge about cause and effect relationship.

The Asian Regional Seminar organized by the UNESCO at Bangkok in 1970 defined population education as "an educational programme which provided for a study of the population situation in the family, community, nation and world for the purpose of developing in the people national and responsible attitudes and behaviour towards that situation." According to Stephen Viedeeman population education is "an educational process which assists persons: (a) to learn the probable causes and consequences of population phenomena for themselves and their community (including the world), (b) to define for themselves and their communities, the nature of the problems associated with population processes and characteristics, and (c) to assess the possible effective means by which society as a whole as an individual can respond to and influence these processes in order to enhance the quality of life now as in future.

The NCERT document (1987) has aptly enunciated, "By doing so they are expected to develop national attitude towards the desirable size and structure of our population and the quality of life in their respective family. They are also expected to appreciate and promote the development of small family norms in the society. The acceptance of observance of small family norms depends a great deal on inculcation of commitment on the part of students." Proper education is, therefore, felt essential to develop right attitudes amongst the vast population, which is to enter the fertility age group after a few years. Such education can enable the young people to know the actual facts and position of our country in particular and of the world in general which will motivate them with a desire to adopt small family norms.

Urban Local Bodies can do the following:

(a) Educating the youth about population growth so that they understand the implications of small family norms in their life.
(b) Creating understanding and a spirit in the youth about population education so that they spread the message to people.
(c) Youth after getting education can work in the

community to remove doubts among the people about population control.

(d) Youth can convince families about quality of life, which can be possible only with small family.

(e) Prepare charts, video films etc. for educating students and people about population education.

(f) Arrange debates and discussions on various issues of population education.

(g) Dissemination of information about population Education.

(h) Prepare groups of youth to promote population education.

PROMOTING HEALTH EDUCATION

The most important aim of Health Education is to alter behaviour, which may have directly or indirectly influence occurrence and spread of diseases in a given cultural setting. A culturally relevant health education programme can be planned only after understanding the behaviour in all its manifestations. One of the best definitions of Health Education was offered by Wood in 1926: "Health Education is the sum of experiences which favourably influences habits, attitudes and knowledge relating to individual, community, and racial health.[9]

Different authorities have differently viewed the aims of health education. According to one source:[10]

> "The aim of health education is to help people achieve health by their own actions and efforts. Health education begins therefore with the interest of people in improving their condition of living, and aims at developing a sense of responsibility for their own health betterment as individuals and as members of families, communities or government."

Another source highlights that, "Health education aims at promoting the greater possible fulfillment of inherited powers of the body and the mind and the happy adjustment of individual to society. It is the educational approach to health problem and as such is concerned with practical measures for the promotion of health and the control and treatment of disease."[11]

Unfortunately, the experts and development planners have failed to improve the lives of the people as they don not understand properly the science to communicate effectively with each other or with the people they are trying to help. Most of the people in authority today, who are guiding the people in this field, have not realized the urgency of such education and the benefit it can generate; consequently governments have not taken any substantial steps in this direction.

Health education does to mean merely removal of ignorance. On the contrary, it involves four important things:

(1) It provides a person with appropriate knowledge to enjoy decent health and also the knowledge about the occurrence and spread of disease thus enabling him to adopt relevant preventive measures;
(2) It creates in him an interest in his own health and well-being;
(3) It even creates in him an interest for the health of other members of his family as well as of those living in his surrounding; and
(4) It creates in him a desire to support health education programmes in his area.

Besides, Health Education should make the people understand the benefits that they can derive from modern medicine. K.S. Sanjive, Professor of Medicine has said:

> "It will not be an exaggeration to say that the paramount step in the effort to take modem medicine to every comer of the country and every citizen is health education. Health education in its widest sense of getting every one to understand what modem medicine can do to diminish disease and death and to be properly motivated to utilize this knowledge in their daily lives, requires the simple quality of sincerity more

than highly specialized techniques."[12]

Neglect of health education is one of the main reasons why scientific medicine is not taking root in the country and people are steeped in ignorance and superstition.

ESSENTIALS OF HEALTH EDUCATION

Health education would be possible only if the health educator and the receiver are in constant dialogue with each other. It is not wholly correct that the purpose of health education is to manipulate the receiver. What might be more appropriate is a circular diagram in which the parties to the "Communication Contract" as it is sometimes called, function dually as senders and receivers. This model would avoid the possibilities of misinterpretation. We know that even well planned campaigns can end in failures if there is no proper monitoring or feedback to make sure that the wrong effect is not being created by the communicator, however innocently.

In a democratic society, the dynamic power, which impels governments to action, is the voice enlightenment of the people. People can only pressurize their executive or legislative machinery to undertake suitable health measures when they themselves are aware of the means of warding off disease and promotion of positive health. This knowledge (Health Education) is therefore a pre-condition and prerequisite to creating the demand for health and setting the pace of implementation of environmental sanitation and the total health policy.

FUNCTIONS OF HEALTH EDUCATION PROGRAMME

No health education programme can function in isolation. A health education programmes have to be an integral part of various other development programmes. Functionally, a health education programme should aim at bringing about the following change.

1. A Change in Knowledge

The most important need which health education programme can serve is to provide appropriate knowledge about health and diseases to the people. This knowledge should be provided in such a way that the recipients do not find it hard to accept it. How to provide this knowledge in an acceptable way? This is the first challenge faced by a health educator. Meaningful responses are relatively easier to learn than the meaningless ones. The health educator can do a lot better by making his demands on the response of receivers, which are meaningful. For instance, the health educator who gives a big lecture to the mother on the value of practicing family planning without indicating its benefits to her as an individual would be showing inadequate understanding of this principle, for she has to look into her own benefits first. Vigorous efforts would be required to proliferate suggestions that are realistic and meaningful.

2. A Change in Attitude

A change in attitude is possible only when the new knowledge that is offered is acceptable to the recipients. Its utility should also be well known to them. Normally, provision of appropriate knowledge should lead to formation of positive attitudes not only towards a person's won health but also towards the health of other members of the community.

3. A Change in Behaviour

Once positive attitudes are formed, these must reflect in the behaviour of the recipients. They should not only become mindful of their past behaviour but should also avoid doing things which can in any way influence occurrence or spread of diseases.

4. A Change in Habit

The change in the behaviour of the recipients must lead to habit formation. A habit can be formed only when the behaviour becomes repetitive. If proper habits are formed, not only the individuals concerned but the whole community will be benefited. Habit formation, however, is a slow process and it has been well said, that 'habits die hard'.

The persuasive communicator or health educator should be interested both in the long-range effects of his messages and in their initial effects. As a matter of fact, he should be interested in turning the learned responses into habitual ones. What are the other principles that guide the establishment of a response? First, the probability of response will increase with the increase in the number of rewarded repetitions. As long as the stimulus with reinforcement following each correct response is not adequately repeated, it will not become a habitual response. Many messages are short-lived because of lack of reinforcement and are likely to become extinct. Second, in order to establish habit patterns, it would be necessary to have a shorter interval between response and reward. Third, habit formation is easier when stimuli are presented in isolation. A nutrition message when unaccompanied by another message such as sanitation message facilitates habit formation. Fourthly, timely increase in reinforcement will further strengthen habit formation. Fifth, receiver's original level of motivation will also influence her habit formation. The mother having a better level of motivation from the beginning will find habit formation much easier. Sixth, providing timely information about receiver performance, would lead to further improvement in performance. Providing selective information to a mother on the positive aspects of her performance will also improve her performance. Thus, communication of health ideas can yield the desired result if the above principles are followed religiously.

5. A Change in Customs

Acquisition of positive attitudes leading to appropriate habit formation must sooner or later, evolve into customs. Only when a substantial number of people in a given cultural setting start behaving in a customary manner, one can say the behaviour has become a part of their customs.

Don Palmer in his article "Social Health: A True Story, Culture and Tradition as Medicine" in the Daily Tribune dated 26th January 2000, rightly stresses the need of health education. Modem urban life, devoid of the goodness of social health, can be particularly tough for young indigenous inhabitants of developed countries. Some kill themselves, while many more drift into drugs, alcohol and crime. Now a prison programme is helping in rehabilitation of aboriginal offenders by reintroducing them to their cultural traditions."

It needs to be re-emphasized that health education is a slow process and that it precedes gradually, a part of the process may get established without any problem but additional efforts may be required to complete the whole process. This process may be directed towards the following important programmes:

(a) Personal hygiene;
(b) Knowledge of modem medicine i.e., use of health services;
(c) Nutrition;
(d) Mental health;
(e) Prevention of communicable diseases;
(f) Care of children;
(g) Environmental sanitation;
(h) Human physiology;
(i) Life style diseases;
(j) Education about Alcohol and drugs.

Health education must be imparted keeping in mind latest developments in the field of health. Life is changing fast and the individuals must be educated in the new technology, its role and limitations. Mr. V. Tatochenko, a member of the WHO Expert Panel on Maternal and Child Health in his Article on "Education for Health" said, "Rapid changes in life styles and the evolution of views on health and diseases call for new departures in health education. A quick glance of health education material of even one generation ago will show how fast it tends to get out of date. Medical facts, it has been estimated, get outdated within a decade or so. Effective health education, therefore, requires a continuous stream of knowledge, development of the people's ability to absorb it, and decisions taken on the basis of a constantly changing body of information.[13]

ADULT EDUCATION

Education holds the key to development and is vital for the stability and maturity of a democratic country. All our scriptures and Plans emphasize the positive correlation between education and development. Ministry of HRD, in its Annual Report on the Department of Education rightly stressed the need of Education. To quote, "Literacy is now accepted as an indispensable component of Human Resource Development. It is an essential tool of communication and learning, for acquiring and sharing of knowledge and information, a precondition for an individual's growth and for national development." Swami Vivekanada, attached great importance to Education. He rightly felt that the only service to be done for our people is to give them education to develop their individuality. They are to be given ideas and their eyes are to be opened to what is going on around them and they will work out their salvation.[14]

The challenge of Education, a Document of the Ministry of HRD, rightly observes that it is also a truism that the nation would not move towards the twenty-first century on two legs unless illiteracy is banished and a universal learning environment is created.[15]

Therefore, there is a great need to remove illiteracy from the country through Adult Education and effective elementary Education System.

According to 10th Plan, there was a considerable degree of awareness of the importance of adult education in the pre-independence period though efforts at adult education during this period were modest. This led to the gradual emergence at the policy level of the view that the State must shoulder the primary responsibility in this regard. The strategy followed immediately after Independence and in successive five-year Plans to provide education to the masses made a distinction between universalisation of elementary education (UEE) and adult education. Overriding priority was given to primary education on the assumption that the expansion of primary education would automatically take care of problems of illiteracy. It was only in 1977-78 that the government decided to accord due weightage to adult education along with the programme of UEE, and the National Adult Education Programme (NAEP) was launched on 2 October 1978. For the first time, adult education was put on the agenda of the nation and thereby made central to the development approach that was pursued. However, the NAEP was not very successful because it was traditional, honorarium-based, hierarchical and government-funded and controlled.

RATIONALE

The Basic questions, which need answers, are:- What is the need for it? Would these efforts yield positive benefits? If yes, what are these benefits? Let us examine them.

(a) Essential to Develop Personality and Status in the Society

Illiterate people are exploited by vested interests in many ways. They feel humiliated in the presence of educated people. Thus, education is essential to create confidence in them and to get a rightful place in the society. This is more significant in case of females as their status can be improved through literacy and thus can become catalytic in the solution of inter-connected problems.

(b) Vital for the Success of Development Programmes

Development Programmes engaged in Socio-economic Development, has not been a great success in India both at the union and State levels. The most important cause of the less success of these programmes has been the illiteracy and ignorance of the people. It has been rightly said that "there is adequate evidence that adult education can and has to be used as an instrument for the bulk of the population which may have never been to school in order to educate them about the programmes of family welfare, hygiene, immunization and child-care. On the other hand, the correlation between illiteracy and high infant mortality, high rate of growth of population, female infanticide and poverty has also been established."[16]

(c) Necessary to make People's Participation a Reality

All our five year plan sand other documents suggest the need of people's participation to strengthen democratic values and traditions, From he point of view of political participation, which is the bed-rock of democracy, adult education has been accorded to play a vital role.[17]

(d) Supports Efficiency in Work through Skill Development

Literate people can pick up skills at a faster rate and thus can support productivity and efficiency in work, an essential pre-requisite for national development.

(e) Makes General Life Interesting and Useful

Literacy can provide newness of life as it opens new vistas in the life of the people. Literate people feel independent and can come out of boredom of life. Besides, literacy takes away people from superstitions and social evils.

HUMAN RIGHTS

All human beings are born free and equal in dignity and rights. The inherent dignity of all members of the human family is the foundation of freedom and justice and peace in the world as given in the Universal declaration of human rights in its preamble. Human rights are the moral claims, which are inalienable and inherent in all human individuals by virtue of their humanity alone. These are the rights of all human beings, because they are born in human family. The concept of human rights and the human rights movement is getting more and more impetus in today's social and political background because it is now universally accepted need that human rights are essential in human lives and hence they must be protected.[18]

An analysis of human rights indicates that these are theoretically sound and promise a decent life to everyone born on this earth. However, majority of the people lacked the knowledge of these rights. The vested few exploited the majority making a life of hell for the majority. The main reason of this has been found to be ignorance. The need is to hammer these rights into the minds of people though education. That is why education has become the main instrument of people to know their rights and methods to safeguard them and in case of violation how to get justice. This education is the key to the achievement of these human rights; enlightened citizenship is the need of today to enjoy decent life.

Today humanity binds us together because the global society has created oneness of mankind. Human rights and their co-relative human duties are founded on eternal and universal human values and ideals transcending all man made boundaries, civilizations cultural or geographic. In times of social, political and economic globalization, traditional values are being questioned and challenged and so education as a social institution is confronted with new challenges in respect to the view of man, one's perception of knowledge and the educational aims and the vision of good life and values and its substantive features. The goal of elevation of man's awareness and consciousness, and of enlightenment of his soul with a view of making a new harmonious multi-cultural world order and a more human civilization requires a synthesis of varieties of cultural and religious diversities of materialism with spiritualism and of the values, ideals and the spirit of all major religions of the world. This further underlines harnessing of every branch of knowledge and the union of moral and secular values with constitutional and legal norms. Revival of the duty-oriented society, a spiritual basis and balancing of human rights and duties as co-relatives and spiritual regeneration of the entire human life through education in a wider sense, can pave the way for a harmonious, just and peaceful global order. Moral and spiritual source of rights and duties enjoins tenacious pursuit of worthy ideals and human values.[19]

The term 'human rights' is commonly used to denote rights, which every human being is entitled to enjoy by virtue of being a human being, and for no other reason. All cultures and societies throughout their history have been involving conceptions of rights, which they held sacrosanct. Various states in their legal systems and constitutions have incorporated rights, which are inviolable. While the contemporary conceptualization of human rights which the

Universal Declaration of Human Rights and its accompanying Covenants embody has drawn on the rich legacy of the past, it is distinguished by its universality, by the fundamental principle that all human rights are meant to be enjoyed by all human beings, anywhere in the world.

TRAINING IN DEVELOPMENT ADMINISTRATION

Lack of Interest among Executive Officers in Development Activities

Executive Officers being too busy in their routine activities do not take keen interest in promoting and reviewing urban participatory development. They should be sensitized and made to understand the importance of this scheme. They complain that they have no adequate funds and it is not the scheme of municipality but of SUDA. We must remove such feelings from their mind.

Development Administration

Development is a process of growth in the direction of modernity, especially towards nation-building and socio-economic progress. It has been stressed, "development is the rational process of organizing and carrying out prudently conceived and staffed programmes or projects as one would organize and carry out military or engineering operations".

According to K.S. Dadzie, United Nations Director-General for Development and International Economic Cooperation, "The final aim of development must be the constant increase of the well-being of the entire population on the basis of its full participation in the process of development and a fair distribution of the benefits there from".

Thus, the main aim of development should be to enrich the quality of life. Dr. T. Adeoya Lambo, Deputy Director-General, WHO, in his article 'Towards Justice in Health' in World Health (July, 1979) has rightly said:

> "What is happening around us shakes our complacency, challenges our faith in human progress and imbues us with an intense feeling of shame, doubt

and guilt. In a world where gigantic scientific and phenomenal technological achievements command our admiration, and almost fetish acceptance, we are witnessing an intolerable degradation of man. Our pride in belonging to a generation that, for the first time since the genesis of man, has set foot on another planet cannot, however, disguise the awful truth that it may be easier to travel to the moon than to erase from the surface of the earth the image of inevitable poverty, human exploitation, injustice and the degradation of human welfare."

The people inhabiting the developing world expect their Governments to pull them out of the morass of distressing under development. This could be possible provided the efforts of the Governments are comprehensive, selective, coordinated and sustained. Besides, timely action backed by a strong will and determination at all decision-making and operational levels can change the complexion of our socio-economic scene.

To handle the tasks of socio-economic development, development administration was employed based on development planning which relates to a "teleological-determined manipulation of policy measures and instruments devised so as to stimulate the authors of the socio-economic scene to act in the way most conducive to the achievement of the national socio-economic development objectives and goals."[20]

Development Administration took its birth in 1960's to project development, but it's meaning was interpreted differently by different scholars.

Let us now define development administration:

Development administration, according to J.N. Khosla, "connotes the totality of administrative processes involved in developmental activities."[21]

George Gant defines the concept, "development administration is that aspect of public administration in which the focus of attention is on organizing and administering public agencies in such a way as to stimulate and facilitate defined programmes of social and economic progress. It involves the adaptation and the application of management skills directly to the development process."[22]

According to Edward W. Weidner, "Development administration is concerned with maximizing innovation for development."[23]

He defines innovation for development as "the process of planned or intended change in the direction of modernity or nation-building and socio-economic change."[24]

The analysis of the definitions reveals that development administration has two important constituents, development of administration and administration of development. In this context, Fred W. Riggs very aptly remarks: "The reciprocal relatedness of these two sides involves a chicken and egg type of causation. Administration cannot normally be improved very much without changes in the environmental constraints (the infrastructure) that hamper its effectiveness; and the environment itself cannot be changed unless the administration of developmental programmes is strengthened."[25]

ESSENTIALS OF DEVELOPMENT ADMINISTRATION

Development administration, to be effective and efficient, needs to have the following ingredients:

I. Administrative Innovation

Reorganization of administrative structures and procedures is essential to weed out impediments though innovation, Administration innovation is the sine qua non-for development administration. Susanne MacGregor in an article, 'Urban Innovations: The London Experience',[26] rightly mentions the need 'Life Cycle' of innovation to improve services.

A 'Life Cycle' of Innovations is assumed, which involves:

(1) Conception;
(2) Adoption;
(3) Early trial and error;
(4) Mature implementation and reutilization;

Dominance, and

(5) Replacement by Newer forms.

2. People's Participation

It is essential to make use of the potential energy of the people through their involvement. T.K. Moulik opines that "participation in development process implies stimulation individuals to take initiative and mobilizing people to work for overall societal development." To quote ILO, "Participation involves collectively organized and continued efforts by the people themselves in setting goals, pooling resources together and taking actions which aim at improving their living conditions."

3. Definite Policies, Programmes and Projects

Formulation of development goals and policies precisely reflecting the need of the people is essential.

4. Monitoring

There is a need of monitoring and evaluation to locate problems and inject improvements for consistent growth and development.

5. Use of Modern Management Techniques

Using modern management techniques for optimizing personnel, a financial and material resource is essential.

6. Achievement Orientation

The emphasis should be on achievement and not mere paper planning.

7. Commitment and Dedication

These are essential to development Commitment and dedication too can provide extra power to development and are an insurance against possible fallout.

Development administration could not achieve much in developing countries. It has become a fashion to name development administration to old administrative structures without introducing changes. The same personnel with the old administrative apparatus are implementing development programmes with utter failures, resulting in the wastage of human, material and financial resources. These remarks have been based upon a number of evaluation studies conducted by the author.

In addition, they must follow the standards of:

If the administrative apparatus of the country is to be rendered safe for posterity, the civil service must give a better account of itself by standing up for the basic values of an honest and efficient administration. But what are the prospects for such a thing happening? These are not bright at all, considering the 'culture of compromise' that is fast spreading among the rank and file of civil servants, high and low. Battered by politicians and power brokers, even the best among them are unable to stand up to the mounting pressures, particularly in the absence of public support and backing. Some of them may yet stand up and be counted, provided they can count upon the support of the people they seek to serve. In this context S.S. Jain has rightly raised the questions: who will enforce norms on the Ministers and how? What do they care for the Secretaries and Heads of Departments? Reportedly, a former Central Minister (Personnel) once said at a meeting "when they appoint Secretaries they are not looking for genius or brilliance, but for the principal quality of a domestic servant-loyalty."[27] Whatever the ministers may have to say, a public servant is committed to the Constitution and the flag, not to a political master. One hopes the civil servants would act with courage, which alone can serve them as also the nation in the present day climate of low ethics and high corruption. In spite of the enactment of laws, rules and regulations to ensure impartiality, honesty and devotion among the civil service, there still remains a vast area of administrative discretion which cannot be supervision from above," says Otto Kirchheimer, "can be as effective as an automatic control on the minds of those possessing it and creating standards of efficiency as well as honesty. Any deviation from the common standards under such circumstances is likely to be discovered sooner or later and rooted out."[28]

In the words of M.C. Canny, in all such areas "They must answer to their own consciences, to their own sense of dignity and pride, to the opinions of their fellowmen and, above all, to their devotion, to their own honest effort to define the total welfare and to serve it."[29] The group of civil servants must be imbued with the ideals of service. It was rightly mentioned by Garner "no society can reach heights of greatness unless, in all fields critical to its growth and creativity, there is an ample supply of dedicated men and women."[30] Administrators at all levels to make the garden of administration fragrant and worthwhile must imbibe the ideals of ethics enshrined in our valuable scriptures of all religions. The administrators of this garden will take care of all the seedlings with interest and dedication. Swami Vivekananda has put beautifully the ideals of service, which must be practiced by the public servants.

The foremost characteristics required among the civil servants are impartiality and consistency in the transaction of public business. Civil servants are required to be completely impartial to avoid corruption and favoritism; civil servants must maintain the dignity and authority of the public office. They must meticulously implement the policies and programmes as laid down in laws, regulations and rules.

There is a need to develop good administrative traditions, which may impel civil servants to perform their activities impartially to keep the administration above board. The civil servants at higher levels of administration must set standards of independence and impartiality through constant practice. The personnel at lower echelons in the administration would imbibe such standards consciously or unconsciously.

Each official on his appointment swears solemnly to perform, in all loyalty, discretion and conscience, the functions entrusted to him and to discharge these functions and regulate his conduct with the interest of the organization alone in view. The practice of these principles must be inculcated through the development of professional standards.

An allied requirement of promoting impartiality is the necessity of developing and maintaining a national outlook. It involves, on the part of the civil service, willingness to try to understand and be tolerant of different points of view, different cultural patterns, and different work habits. It also entails willingness to work without prejudice or bias with persons of all regions, religions and cultures.

It involves conduct of the highest type, and exercise of judgment and restraint in all expressions of view, whether public or private; any expression, which could be construed as biased or intolerant, particularly in respect of regional interests or political issues with which the organization is confronted, must be scrupulously avoided.

The loyalty or impartiality requires a positive attitude, i.e., to act with dedication divorced from emotions and prejudices. The Roman Emperor, Marcus Aurelius, wrote about his duties in memorable words, which are quoted below and must be imbibed by civil servants in the present day:

(a) Do what comes to hand with correct and natural dignity and with humanity, independence and justice, and allow your mind freedom from all other considerations.

(b) Human Aspects

Skills to improve motivation to increase the productivity of the personnel working in the organization.

(c) Organizational Aspects

The knowledge of the organization, the use of records, communication skills, etc.

We can emphatically say that training of employees and beneficiaries of local self-govt. is the most important as this can lubricate their potential energies and change this into kinetic energy. Keeping this in view Govt. of India has made education and training as an integral component of all urban schemes.

The term 'governance' means more than government or management. It refers to the relationship not only between governments and state agencies but also between government and communities and social groups. 'Governance' is a broader and more inclusive term than government. It encompasses the activities of a range of groups-political, social, and governmental-as well as their inter-relationships. Urban Local Governance thus subsumes the operation of local governments, their relationships with societies within which they operates.

The term 'governance' is used to describe various processes of participatory development. 'Good Governance' implies simplicity in rules and regulations, managerial efficiency, adaptiveness, responsiveness and transparency, which need to be followed in a participatory and consultative process of development. This broader meaning of the term largely stems from the fact that governments at all levels have not been able to fulfill the goals of human development. In the context of urban areas, the inability of the local governments to cope-up with the provision of basic services and infrastructure is starkly visible.

ADMINISTRATIVE ETHICS

Ethics is the moving spirit of a welfare state. All the problems emanating today in a family or society or Government are the product of ignoring ethics for selfish motives. Ethical government may appear to be harsh for temporary period, but this is the only alternative for a permanent beneficial government.

"One could argue that ethical behaviour should in itself be rewarding. However, there are tangible benefits well. Business is built on relationship with the suppliers, customers, employees, and other groups. The strength of these relationships is largely a function of the amount of trust the parties have in each other ...Studies have shown that the firms which maintain ethic standards perform much better than others due to the good relationships they have with their suppliers, customers, employees and general public. Thus, ethics are cornerstone of business success."[31]

We get a moral government by creating those conditions within which a moral government can operate. This is done by making it possible for officials to acquire the necessary traits and by the practice of the same. An exemplary public servant, to be specific, is not simply one who obeys the laws and behaves within the confines of law but is also one who strives for a moral government. Such is the duty of those who wish to be involved in the difficult and complex world of government. This is the essence and basis of a moral state.[32]

Public life is in a desperate state today, with vice-regal regalia dominating it with its fierce ferocity and crushing criminality, sounding the death-knell of ethicality, morality, and value-system. There is dire need to save it. Public men-at whatever station of life they function -must be men for the public; leaders must lead; and, most importantly, politicians must stop 'politiking'. Public opinion-must be built up against acceptance and tolerance of unethical behaviour and action.

ASPECTS OF TRAINING

Training Contents For Executive Officers

Besides telling them about the schemes and other new development, they were given training in management as most of them were recently promoted. Their training included principles of management like:

Planning

The workings out in broad outline the things that need to be done and method to be adopted to accomplish the purpose of the public policy. Public administration has to play positive role in developing countries.

Organization

The establishment of the formal structure of authority through which the work is sub-divided, arranged, defined and coordinated for the defined objective.

Staffing

The whole personnel, bringing in and training the staff, and maintenance of favourable conditions of work.

Directing

The continuous task of making decisions and embodying them in specific and general orders and instructions, and thus providing the necessary guidance.

Co-ordinating

The all-important duty of interrelating the various aspects of administration.

Reporting

Keeping those, to whom the executive is responsible, informed as to what is going on, which includes keeping the agency itself and its subordinates informed through records, research and inspection.

Budgeting

All that goes with budgeting in the form of fiscal planning, accounting and control.

Then they were given intensive training in building relationships with the people sine qua-non-for local govt.

CREATING HARMONIOUS RELATIONSHIPS WITH THE PEOPLE

Public administration and citizen are intimately related to each other as the existence of one without the other is not possible in a civilized society. The harmonious relationship depends upon the sincerity, earnestness and cooperation between the two. To quote Robson:

> "The achievement of good relations between the government and the public is a matter which does not by any means depend solely on the conduct of civil servants and politicians. It depends equally on the attitude of citizens groups, corporations, associations of all kinds and, indeed, of all unofficial bodies to public authorities. If we want public servants to behave well towards us, we must behave well towards them. Moreover, we must if politicians and civil servants are held in low esteem, if their work is decried, if abuse and invective is poured on them continuously, if loose and unsubstantial allegations are made about their incompetence, dishonesty, laziness and indifference to the public interests, it is unlikely that officials will develop or display qualities of integrity, industry and

public spirit."[33]

Good citizens administrative relationship would:

(a) Encourage people's participation- a sine qua non for development and modernization;
(b) Kindle the potential energy of the citizens into kinetic energy to accelerate development;
(c) Supplement the efforts of the government in the conduct of its affairs;
(d) Strengthen the values of democracy in the minds and spirit of the people;
(e) Enlist respect in the constitution, which is rooted in people's sovereignty;
(f) Develop bonds of friendship and good will between citizens and administration, and vice-versa; and
(g) Avoid social unrest, tensions, violence and other social upheavals, which have become the order of the day.

Administration is never something apart from people and their needs; rather it is the means by which these needs are met and the administrator who thinks of his organization as something apart from the community will fail to recognize significant problems of the citizens and the administration will not be in a position to deliver the goods.

ARC has also observed in this very connection:

"If, in the prosperity of the people, lies the strength of a government, it is in their contentment that lies the security and stability of democracy."[34]

PROJECT MANAGEMENT

They were also given training about Project Administration so that they can make new Projects in their cities.

The success of the achievement of goals depends to a great extent upon the success of the implementation of projects. This is the most neglected area in the developing countries. The success of our Five Year and annual plans depends to a substantial extent upon effective project management. In the developing countries, projects are neither properly prepared nor implemented, resulting in the wastage of resources.

Training in leadership, supervisions and communication may follow it.

LEADERSHIP

The success or failure of an organization depends, to a great extent, upon the administrative capability and motivation of its top leadership. Administrative capability is an important means of converting or processing programme inputs into outputs such as goods and services. V.L. Gabriel[35] has mentioned it:

> "What makes the leadership variable so crucial in the implementation process is its dynamic, not passive, quality, i.e., it s capability to act and react on these critical inputs. It is this administrative and transferring quality of leadership that could significantly determine the administrative capability of implementing organization".

According to G.R. Terry:

> "leadership is the activity of influencing people to strive willingly for group objective.

According to F.E. Fiedler:

> "leadership is the 'task of directing and coordinating task relevant group activities".

The attributes that are required in leadership may be briefly summarized as: technical competence, missionary zeal, the capacity to motivate others, the capacity to communicate with others, the ability to get along with people, cultural adaptability, the capacity, to organize and manage, the capacity to inspire confidence in others, patience and dignity. Besides, a leader must believe in the ideals of the organization, be willing to accept hardships and prepared to work in a spirit of service. His ambition and enthusiasm should not be dampened by local conditions, which may not provide him with the necessary facilities.

EROPA has emphasized the following qualities:[36]

First, there are certain specialized fields of knowledge and skill, which are programme-relevant, such as substantive knowledge of engineering the infrastructure programme.

Second, managerial expertise and skills are paramount in effective implementation, coordinating and scheduling work, planning and allocating resources, and so on.

Third, modern administrative leaders need human relations' ability to deal with a major resource in organizational life. Motivating people to perform beyond normal requirements, to instill a strong sense of programme-commitment and integrity and to incite programme personnel to unfetter the suffocating bonds of anachronistic administrative values, traditions and practices are additional requisite skills.

Finally, there are certain 'political' skills required to sustain support and co-operation from the volatile public (legislators and ministers), mass media, and clientele, local, political notables.

SUPERVISION

Planning, communication and supervision are the three main steps in the process of direction. Like every other aspect of organization, supervision is also becoming very complicated and complex. The responsibilities of a supervisor have increased and a good supervisor is expected to have the qualities of head and heart. There is an old saying:

> "which is not inspected is not done". Hence inspection, overseeing and supervision arise in response to needs inherent in the functioning of an organization.

According to J.M. Pfifner,[37] a good supervisor should possess the following eight qualities:

1. Command of job content, i.e., expert knowledge of the work to be done;
2. Personal qualification like integrity; teaching ability, i.e., the ability to communicate his ideas to the workers and make them understand the management's point of view;
3. General outlook, i.e., the supervisor should love his job and be absorbed in it and inspire those under him;
4. Courage and fortitude, i.e., the ability to take decisions and assume responsibility;
5. Ethics and morals, i.e., freedom from vices having social disapprobation;
6. Administrative technology, i.e., the ability to manage.
7. Curiosity, i.e., receptivity to new ideas; and
8. Intellectual ability, i.e., intellectual alertness, etc.

Besides, the qualification and qualities mentioned above, he should be mature enough to take timely action based upon the given situation rather than allowing the situation to deteriorate. For this, it is suggested that training programmes may be arranged frequently for supervisors to equip them in the art and science of supervision.

TRAINING IN COMMUNICATION, COORDINATION AND CONTROL

"Efficient communication is essential to all aspects of effective administration. Staff must be adequately and currently informed about plans, methods, schedules, problems, events and progress. It is necessary that instructions, knowledge, and information be passed on for practical application to all concerned, and that they be so clearly presented as to make misinterpretation or misunderstanding impossible. Proper and adequate communication is not just in one direction. It requires

> two-way passage. Administration must be certain that they know and understand the problems of workers for whom they are responsible. Communications must flow from the bottom upwards, as well as from the top down."[38]

Broadly speaking, communication is the means through which intentions of the programmes are translated to ensure fruitful results. It may even be looked upon as the means by which special information inputs are fed into social systems. It is the means by which behaviour of the personnel engaged in the programme is modified; change is effected, information is made productive and goals are achieved.[39] Barnard has viewed it as the means by which people can be linked together in an organization to achieve the objectives of the programme.[40] Newman and Summer have viewed communication as an exchange of facts, ideas, opinion, or emotions by two or more persons.[41]

PUBLIC RELATIONS

The creation of awareness is integral to social and economic development. The possibility for the power of communication is to liberate the minds and potential of people to critical awareness is real in every field linked to human development and the generation of public will hinges on effective communication of information and ideas that relate to people's needs, aspirations and capacities for progress in thought and action. In this sense, getting development process started is largely the task of information, education and communication through public relations.

Public relation is the establishment of a climate of understanding. It means interpreting the programme of an organization to the public and vice-versa. According to J.L. McCany:

> "Public relations in government is the composite of all the primary and secondary contacts between the bureaucracy and the citizens and all the interaction,

influences and attitudes established in these contacts". According to Harwood:

"Public relations may be defined as those aspects of our personal and corporate behaviour which have a social rather than private and personal significance."[42]

The purpose of public relations is not only to supply information, but also to encourage an understanding and cooperation between the citizens and the public servants. The objectives of public relations should be to increase prestige and goodwill and to protect the life of the organization by safeguarding it against unwarranted attacks as well as to remove the genuine complaints and grievances of the people.

TRAINING TO APOs, COs ETC.

Let us first describes the duties and responsibilities of Assistant Project Officers and Community Organizers, so that we can provide training to them accordingly:

(i) guide and monitor the work of COs;
(ii) prepare city convergence plans based on the community plans and sectoral programmes at district and municipal levels;
(iii) promote integrated and coordinated implementation of UPA convergence plan;
(iv) promote linkages of UBSP structures with the new structures under the 74th CAA.
(v) Mobilize the human and financial resources at the city level;
(vi) Review and approve community action plans; and
(vii) Monitor programme activities at city level (MIS).

COMMUNITY ORGANIZER

(i) facilitating and promoting voluntarism and organizing community structures/groups;
(ii) guiding and assisting the community in need assessment and formulating plans;

(iii) working with the community to implement and monitor the programme;
(iv) liaise with the sectoral departments to establish initial contacts with the community;
(v) facilitating community skill enhancement through interactive experiences;
(vi) organizing community level training and information sharing.

The first emphasis of training of this category should be on Participation of Slum dwellers. Besides they may also trained in those qualities, which are essential for Executive Officers as mentioned earlier.

PARTICIPATORY

Participation development is defined as stimulating productive energies of people, encouraging broader involvement of all people in productive processes and a more equitable sharing of their benefits. It must become more central elements in development strategies and development cooperation.

Participation is an important event that emphasizes the quality of life of local societies as a step towards the realization of self-reliant, sustainable development and social justice. Urban governance is the ideal foundation for improving the quality of life of slum dwellers. The function of government can be improved by participation of slum dwellers. It reflects the people's will more efficiently and the people's confidence in the government rises.

Participation should not be temporary; it must evoke that sustainable up grading of participation quality. For this to happen the basic conditions should be met to facilitate the long-term process of participation and its self-reliant sustain ability. A long-term process of participation mentioned here is: raising the awareness of slum dwellers, forming community groups among them, upgrading their requisite resource management abilities, creating norms or internalizing their mechanisms and improving capabilities for external negotiations.

Following need to be stressed during training:

- Those slum-dwellers have as much of a right as anyone else to participate in governance.
- Those slum-dwellers provide invaluable services to the social and economic life of the city, and their participation in its governance should be viewed not as condescension, but rather as a measure of enhancing the quality and experience of urban living for all.
- That, from the practical angle, through the creation of synergies and through the generation of co-operation and enthusiasm, the difficulties and obstacles that confront urban administrators have a greater chance of being overcome when people's participation in governance is ensured.
- That democratically constituted, empowered Neighbourhood Committees are an effective instrument towards the achievement of this objective.

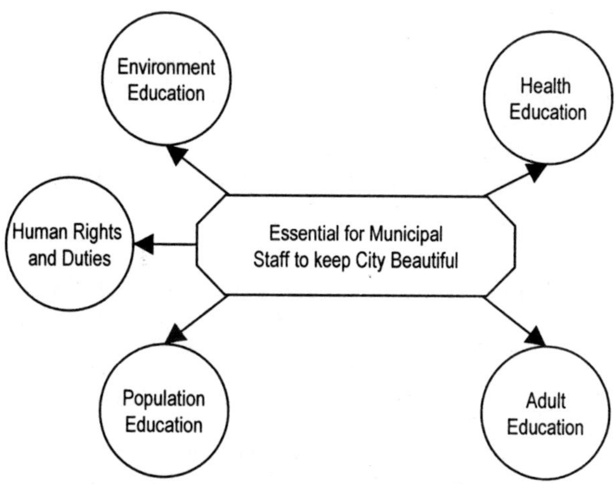

CONCLUSION

Slum development cannot take place until and unless the municipal staff takes interest in them. For this purpose, training to municipal staff is essential, so that they can tackle the problems of slums scientifically.

Notes and References

1. A.R. Tyagi, "Administrative Training: A Theoretical Postulate", International Review of Administrative Science, Vol. XL, No. 2, 1974, p. 157.
2. M. Kantz, Saul, Methodological Note on Appraising Administrative Capability for Development, UN Publication (Sales No. E. 69-II. 4.2), p. 8.
3. Ernest Dale and L.D. Michelon, Modern Management Techniques, Penguin Books, 1974, p. 8.
4. Hames L. Marshall, Development Teaching, New York: 1949, pp.190-306.
5. Hiroshi Makajima, "A Wounded Planet", in World Health January-February 1990, p. 3.
6. Dr. Wilfried Krielsel, "Environment Health in 1990's in World Health, January-February 1990, p. 5.
7. T.R. Badu, Union Minister of Environment and Forests.
8. J.P. Singh, Problems of Population and Sustainable Development in India, in ISPA, June-March 2003, p. 86
9. John J. Hanlon, Principles of Public Health Administrtion , St. Louis, 1960, p. 402.
10. WHO, Technical Report Series, No. 89, p. 4.
11. WHO, *Ibid.*, No. 156, p. 3.
12. K.S. Sanjive, Planning India's Health, Orient Longman, New Delhi, 1971, p. 64.
13. WHO, World Health, Feb.-March 1979, p. 24.
14. Annual Report of the Ministry of HRD, 1992-93, Part I, p. 135.
15. Challenge of Education, p. 93.
16. *Ibid.*, p. 94.
17. *Ibid.*
18. Mrs. Shnehal Fadnovas, Impact of Women's Rights Movement on the Development of Human Rights in South Asian Countries, in Journal of the Institute of Human Rights, Vol. II, No. 1, Jaripatka, Nagpur.
19. R.P. Dhokalia, External Human Values and World Religions, New Delhi, NCERT, 2001, p. 10.
20. UN: Proceedings of the Inter-regional Seminar on Organization and Administration of Development Planning Agencies, Vol., 1, p. 113, (Sales No. E.7411, H.2).
21. Khosla, J.N., "Research in Development Administration', in V.A. Paipanandikar, Ed., Development Administration in India, New Delhi, Macmillan, 1974, p. 217.
22. Gant, George F., "A Note on Application of Development Administration', in J.D. Montgomery and A Smithies, eds., Public

Policy, XV (Cambridge, Harvard Univ. Press, 1966).

23. Weinder, Edward W., 'Development and Innovational Roles', in Weidner (ed.), *op. cit.*, p. 399.
24. *Ibid.*
25. Riggs, F.W., 'The Idea of Development Administration', in Weidner (ed), *op. cit.*, pp. 32-33.
26. MacGregor, Susanne, 'Urban Innovation: The London Experience', Urban India, Vol. XII, No. 1, January-June, 1992, p. 2.
27. The Tribune, March 28, 1990.
28. Kirchhemier, Qtto, 'The Historical and Comparative Background of the Hatch Act', in Public Policy, Cambridge, Mass, 1941, p. 365.
29. Canny, James M.C., The Administration of American Foreign Affairs, 1950, p. 335.
30. Garner, John W., Excellence, New York, Harper and Brothers, 1961, p. 154.
31. Atul Dhingra and M.R.P. Singh, "Ethics is making all the Difference" in Indian management, July 2000.
32. O.P. Dwivedi, "Conclusion: A Comparative Analysis of Ethics, Public and Public Service", James S. Bowman and F.A. Elliston (eds.) Ethics, Government and Public Policy, New York, Greenwood Press, 1988, p. 318.
33. William A. Robson (Ed.), The Civil Service in Britain and France, Hogarth Press, 1956, p. 13.
34. ARC: Interim Report of the A.R.C. on Problem of Redress of Citizens Grievances, p. 7.
35. Gabriel V. Legisias, College of Public Administration, University of Philippines, 'Administrative Capability as a Neglected Dimension in the Implementation of Development Programmes and Project'; Seventh General Assembly and Conference of EROPA on Implementation of the Problem of Archieving Results, October 24-31, 1973, Vol III, pp. 3-14.
36. EROPA: Summary Report of the Seventh General Assembly and Conference on 'Implementation; the Problem of Achieving Results,' Vol. II, pp. 1-8.
37. Pfiffner, J.M., Supervision of Personnel, New York, Prentice Hall, 1958.
38. Goddard, H.A., Principles of Administration Applied to Nursing Service, World Health Organisation, Geneva, 1958, p. 85.
39. Koontz H. and C. O'Donnell, Principles of Management: An Analysis of Managerial Functions, London, McGraw Hill, Kogakusa Ltd., 1972, pp. 538-40.
40. Barnard, Chester I., The Functions of the Executive, Cambridge: Harward University Press, 1968, pp. 226-227.
41. Newman, H.H., C.E. Summer, 'The Process of Management': Concepts, Behaviour and Practice, Englewood Cliffes, N.J. Prentice Hall, 1961, p. 59.
42. Hardwood, Childs L., An Introduction to Public Opinions, *op. cit*, p. 2.

6

Development Administration for Slum Improvement

ASSESSMENT AND IMPACT OF TRAINING TO RCVs

Research Methodology

We have discussed the problems of urban life especially of the people living in Bastis. We have discussed the community-based structures set up under various schemes to improve the life in Bastis. As stated in Chapter V, State Urban Development Authority, Punjab, provided intensive training to all categories of personnel, Volunteers, APOs and Municipal staff. As per the requirement of the scheme, Evaluation of training is to be done to pinpoint problems in different areas of training and suggest remedies so that training system can be improved in future.

We, now spell out the objectives of our study.

To assess the quantity and quality of training imparted to RCVs, EOs, APOs and COs etc. in terms of:

1. Contents;
2. Quality of trainers,
3. Relevance to the participants;
4. Duration;
5. Venue and facilities;
6. Interest and motivation among the participants;

7. To assess the impact of training in promoting group participation to solve their problems;
8. To assess the impact of training in creating awareness about the community resource mobilization;
9. To assess whether the community through RCV/EO/APO/CO has started taking active interest in municipal affairs;
10. To assess whether the training to EO, APO, CO and RCV has motivated them to devote time to improve the living conditions of residents of Bastis;
11. To assess whether municipal staff has devoted some time to deliberate on the problems of Bastis and in preparing master plan for their improvement;
12. To assess whether municipal staff, APO/CO and RCV etc. have helped the members of Bastis in getting the benefit of loan and subsidy from banks and other institutions;
13. To assess whether RCVs have acquired the necessary skill to coordinate with other sectors of development;
14. To asses the overall impact of the training on the improvement of the quality of life of the residents of the Bastis; and
15. To assess the overall impact on the health, hygiene and awareness of the people living in slum areas.

The study was initiated by obtaining views of experts from the UNICEF, Ministry of Urban Affairs, IIPA, Institute of Urban Development, Department of Administrative Reforms and Public Grievances, Government of Indian and World Bank Authority.

We have used all the tools to collect, analyze and interpret our data collected through both secondary and primary sources.

Secondary Data

Based on the advice of experts, the literature available on the subject was screened. Besides, the reports and other relevant studies were also collected from various agencies. These were discussed in the SUDA office in detail. These include:

1. Documents of the Ministry of Urban Development;
2. Documents of SUDA;
3. Documents of UNICEF;
4. General Books;
5. Ninth & Tenth Five Year Plans of GOI and Punjab Government; and
6. Primary Data.

Based on these discussions, five sets of questionnaire were prepared to collect information from various groups involved in urban improvement schemes. These are as follows:

1. Residential Community Volunteers (RCVs) questionnaire consisting of 47 questions.
2. The Members of Neighbourhood Committee (NHCs) questionnaire consisting of 23 questions.
3. E.O./C.O's/A.P.O.'s questionnaire consisting of 18 questions.
4. Community Development Structure (other than RCVs) questionnaire consisting of 19 questions.
5. Beneficiaries questionnaire consisting of 36 questions.

These were discussed among the SUDA experts and then got translated in Punjabi as well so that these can be properly understood. After this, these questionnaires were pre tested at three places.

Observations

Observation, a tool of research, was used extensively. Visits were made to many places to examine personally the extent of progress made through community based structures.

Case study method

In order to understand in depth, case study method has been used. In this context case studies of Rajpura and Ropar were made.

Participatory Observation

The researchers sometimes mixed up with the beneficiaries without disclosing identify to find out real facts.

The Research Methodology adopted was by visiting in permutation and combination to 12 cities (sample) for observations, discussion with officials and non-officials.

Besides NGO's, Health and medical personnel and other prominent persons available were also associated. It was an interesting experience. The meeting in one city generally lasted for 1-2 days. These meetings were arranged by APO, CO's. Informal meetings also followed this, without APO and CO's at few places.

Besides, observations and discussions, survey schedules for different categories of personnel were got completed by outside personnel and NGO's, to get objective assessment.

There were in all 576 Survey Schedules for different categories of personal in 12 cities Surveyed. (Sample)

RCV	207
NHG	084
CDS	102
EO, CO's APO	029
Beneficiary	154
Total	576

Let us discuss the findings of each category.

Elected representatives of Municipalities also show very less interest. There is a need to impact training to them in appreciating the scheme.

Elected Representatives can be made to take interest through:

(i) Intensive Training;
(ii) Equipping them with Ideas to solve local problems;

(iii) Valuing their opinions;
(iv) Recognizing their services.

3. APOs and COs are frustrated on account of:

(a) Low salaries;
(b) Lack of status in municipality;
(c) Long areas to be covered;
(d) More paper work;
(e) Wastage of time in traveling;
(f) No offices in Bastis;

APOs and COs must be compensated adequately:

Terms of Employment

(i) The importance of pay or compensation is of a very great high order for every employee. The standards of living and the social prestige of an employee depend to a great extent on the pay he draws. A man chooses his career on the basis of pay, which he expects to receive.

Mason Haire remarks, "Pay in one form or another, is certainly one of the mainsprings of motivation, in our society."[1] The health and vitality of services depends on the levels of remuneration. Therefore, the salary system must be so designed as to attract, motivate and retain the staff. The tempo of undertaking challenging and arduous tasks by the government can only be accelerated if they have the right number of employees, with the right level of talent and skills, in the right place at the right time, performing the right activities to achieve the right goals.[2] But organizations cannot attract such talented and motivated personnel unless they establish their image as model employers because an organization, which cannot pay its personnel adequately, has not right to exist in the modern world. A model employer need not necessarily offer the highest rates of pay, but should aim at creating such working environments within the enterprise which will induce employees not only to have an economic attachment with the unit but also a sense of involvement and emotional integration with it.[3] The true test of a model employer, in the words of the Third Central Pay

Commission (CPC), should be, "Whether the government is attracting and retaining the personnel it needs and they are reasonably satisfied with the pay and other conditions of service taken as a whole. The fulfillment of this test is an essential prerequisite for the proper functioning of administrative machinery."[4]

Thus, an adequate and sound salary structure together with other working conditions is the. 'sine qua non' for organizational efficiency and effectiveness. Otherwise, as the Administrative Reforms Commission aptly observes, it has been "one of the major factors for strikes, inter-service tensions and rivalries, indifferent attitude to work, poor performance, frustration and low morale of the employees."[5] In other words, the aim of the organizations should be to create and maintain such conditions whereby an employee feels like giving his best, gets satisfaction out of his job and is suitably rewarded. Under such conditions, the money so spent is never wasted. Rather, the employer gets from the people more than what he invests in them.

(ii) Proper planning of work need be done to avoid wastages on non-essential items.

4. APOs and COs lack the following, which need analysis:

(a) No schedule of work, hence very difficult to locate them;
(b) Very less time utilisation;
(c) Lack of basic understanding and rationale of the scheme;
(d) Avoid visiting basties, mostly want to remain in municipalities or at home;
(e) Lack of rapport with the Executive Officer and elected representatives;
(f) Lack of initiative;
(g) No technical support from SUDA as there are no posts of education offices in SUDA;
(h) No attempt at making the use of convergence. Health department people who were keen to help them were not approached;
(i) Lack of review of the programmes;

(j) Most of them return daily to their houses causing casual attitude on their part.

In short, Urban Participatory Development is a challenging task as it is easy to change the mountains them to change the minds of the people. It requires strong determination, dedication, hardwork, goodwill and sympathy among COs who are the agents of change. Therefore, we must ensure that the persons appointed for this job must possess the following qualities:-

(a) missionary zeal;
(b) ability to communicate;
(c) ability to comprehend;
(d) not discouraged by adverse circumstances;
(e) cultural adaptability;
(f) enjoying work job satisfaction. They may be guided by this motto of Swami Vivekananda:
"It is great privilege,
for all of us
to be allowed
to do anything for the world
in helping the world,
we really help ourselves."

On personal discussion with Community Organizer we suggest the following to enhance capability and capacity of Community Organizer.

(a) Refresher training should be given to Community Organizer at State level institute.
(b) Training may be imparted through actual Case Studies where trainees must play an active role through role-playing.
(c) Good instituting may encourage Community Organizer awards to be given at District level functions.
(d) Community Organizer must promote actions, which are realistic and feasible within the constraints faced by the community.

(e) They should build on ideas, concepts and practices that people already have.

(f) They may provide opportunities for dialogue and discussion to allow learner participation and feedback on understanding and implementation.

(g) They should use demonstration to show the benefits of adopting practices.

ROLE OF NHC IN URBAN PARTICIPATORY DEVELOPMENT

Socio-Economic Status of NHG Members

Out of 84 contacted 59 are SC/ST total of all are 84 female. Out of 84 NHG members 7% are above matric. 14% are below matric, 32% are below middle. Majorities of NHG members are married 90%. Most of NHG members are between the age group of 40-60 years. All of the NHG members identify the local problems i.e. 98%. Majorities of NHG members identify the basis of community needs i.e. 98%. All of the NHG members support the action of other agencies 98%. All of the NHG members build the common capacity through training 100%. Majority of NHG members helps the Municipal staff in recovering loans. Most of the NHG member feel that Municipal Council staff is functioning actively. Majority of NHG members regularly attends meetings and discusses for solving common problems of the basti 93%. Majority of NHG members feel that role of M.C./ P.O./Bank Manager/C.O.P.O./APO/CO and Municipal staff as very good 47%. Main problems of the basti are lack of poor status of women 84%, lack of good residential accommodation 57% and lack of sanitation 56%. Overall impact of urban development programme is very good 48%.

A personnel discussion and observation revealed the following:

(1) NHG is an essential institution as it is very near to the families. RCVs have to make all the women living in neighbourhood co-operate in the development of Bastis. Since many of the families have difference on various counts, RCVs with the

help of Community Organizer should first solve their problems and make the NHG and ultimately NGC harmonious.

(2) NHG members have no faith in some of the RCV who try to get benefit only for them. Community Organizer should remove such doubts and create confidence in them.

(3) Neighbourhood problems can be solved only by NHG and not by outsiders. Therefore, they should be given training in appropriate technology.

(4) Neighbourhood Group, so far, is depending on Government and are not moving towards self-reliance.

(5) Community Organizers because of lack of time have failed to motivate them to participate.

(6) They lack the aptitude for development, which need be included by COs.

We can thus say that development is a challenging and arduous task, which require the dedication, hard work and sincerity on the part of the Community Organizers. Once the inertia of the members of NHG is removed, they can accelerate the momentum of development. They need be properly motivated.

On the basis of the above definitions, it can be said that motivation is a tendency, which keeps a person attentively and purposefully engaged to achieve his formulated goals. Thus, a sense of commitment occurs only when the enterprise becomes a perpetual vehicle for the satisfaction of the dominant needs of the employees, so long as the employee strives fully to achieve the goals of the enterprise. From the above discussion, it is clear that motivation as such cannot be observed, rather it is a concept derived to cover a number of relationships having their immediate point of origin within the organism.

It needs stimulating leadership of APO and CO.

Stimulating Leadership

The success of failure on an organization depends to a great extent, upon the administrative capability and motivation of its top leadership. Administrative capability is an important means of converting or processing programmes an important means of converting or processing programmes inputs into outputs such as good and services. It has been mentioned by V.L. Gabriel that, "what makes the leadership variable so crucial in the implementation process is its dynamic, not passive quality, i.e., its capability to act and react on these critical inputs. It is this administrative and transferring quality of leadership that could significantly determine the administrative capability of implementing organizations."[6]

Administrative capability is "the capacity to obtain intended results through organization."[7] Katz says, "Administrative capability for development involves the ability to mobilize, allocate and combine the actions that are technically needed to achieve development objectives."[8]

Leaders must be the persons with vision, initiative and desire to achieve the operational goals with dedication and perseverance. In the words of Shri Jawaharlal Nehru, "No administrator, I suppose, or any one else for the matter of that, can really do first class work without a sense of function, without some measures of a crusading spirit. I am doing this, I have to achieve this, as a part of great movement in a big cause. That gives a sense of function not the sense of individual, narrow approach of doing a job in an office for a salary or wage, something connected with your life's outlook or anything, perhaps being interested, as people inevitably are, on one's personal preferment in that particular work."[9]

The greatest efficiency and productivity will flow from the efforts of those who find satisfaction in their work and conditions of services, who sense an awareness of usefulness of their function, who feel encouraged to move ahead and to meet new challenges who perceive their working environment as one in which high standards of performance are maintained and reward and not one in which indolence and incompetence can be ignored or even protected and rewarded. Motivation can do miracle as a motivated worker can achieve more than an expert with no motivation. Manager must, therefore, devote considerable time and effort in planning for and achieving high levels of motivation and morale. In such a situation, we would achieve goal congruence, i.e., identity between the individual goals and the organizational goals.

Living together is a beginning.
Keeping together is progress.
Working together is success.

Effective Communication

Communication can promote motivation through informed participation. According to Le Thaer, the administration of any Organization can be accomplished only through communication...Poor communication, Poor administration...Administration is totally dependent upon communication for its execution, and the success with which an administrator can communicate determines, in large part, the success with which he may administer his organization.

ROLE OF CDS IN IMPROVING COMMUNITY STRUCTURE AFTER TRAINING

Out of 102 female respondents approached 61 belonged to SC/ST (60%), as far as education is concerned 36% are illiterate, 24% are educated till Vth standard and a few around 8% are educated upto matric. 95% respondents are married, 6 respondents are widows and the rest unmarried. Most of the respondents belong to the age group of 25-40 years, about 23% belong to age group of 40-60 years and the rest are below 25 years of age.

The respondents around 89% of them are aware of the agencies like health departments, for fulfillment of community needs while about 11% seem to be unaware of the same. 90% of the respondents extended their fullest possible help in identification of beneficiaries and further imparting training to them. While 11% respondents showed no interest. 99% of the respondents have extended their help in conducting community survey for economic benefits.

30% of the respondents help in preparing community plans proposals for effective wards development in their community for getting benefits while 20% showed no interest. 90% of the CDS members walk hand to hand with the CO/APO and extend help in UPE cell meeting for ensuring repayment of loans by personal visits and holding talks with said beneficiary (defaulter) while 10% do not take any pains for such work as they have small children in the family to look after or too much involvement in domestic household chores.

72% of the members take pains to create small assets in the community of low income areas so that some income can be generated for community benefit while 28% are unmindful of the same. Members (85%) feel that the major incumbancy in their basti is unemployment, 60% feel problem of sanitation, 48% feel that women's status is not up to the mark 46% feel there are lack of educational facilities like anganwadis, in their area while 40% seem unenthusiastic for development and 53% feel lack of good residential accommodation. The CDS (46%) feel that the impact of implementation of SJSRY scheme has been good (43%), 11% feel it very good.

Based on discussion and observation, we mention here the following issues and problems which need attention of MOUD, State Government and SUDA.

1. CDS is an apex Organisation in the overall process of urban participatory development but one feels sad when it is found that CDS either does not exist in many places or lying defunct or not registered. APOs and COs should give top priority in getting the formation of active CDS because only through this agency, other agencies take NHG, RCV can be made functional. Macro-approach is essential to reach mirco-level.
2. It was mentioned at many places that the funds allocated to CDS are very meager. Funds need be increased so that activities entrusted to them can be carried out successfully.
3. APOs and COs have not been active in providing technical know how and appropriate technology to CDS so that they can improve the quality of life

in Bastis. The members of CDS are to be given the ideas continuously as they are entrenched in poverty and have lost the ability inherent in them to think about their potentiality.

4. Members of CDS do not attend the meetings regularly. No record of the meeting is kept. The activities mostly remain in paper.
5. One of the important activity of the CDS is planning. They lack the art and science of planning in which they can contribute a lot. Since the scheme is aimed at to make them self-reliant. APOs and Cos should impart them training in planning. They may invite some experts team the area, may be retired people who want to give voluntary services, to give them the training in planning.
6. CDS is enamused with the idea that it is a Government scheme and Government would provide all facilities to them while the actual fact is that they have to develop themselves with little support of Government as a catalytic agent.
7. CDS has no proper place to conduct meetings. There is a need to provide such a place where posters, literature can be placed. The place can serve as a pivotal point for the exchange of ideas about the development of the area.
8. Members of CDS can form committees so that time can be saved.
9. Executive Officer/Municipal Staff should address the CDS once in a month.
10. Elected members of municipality should develop a given liaison with them as the purpose of both is the same - to make the city beautiful.
11. The administrative structure and arrangements of CDS is not known to majority of its functionaries from the NHG. It is, therefore, essential to make CDS active and purposeful. Theoretically, it is very sound but in practice, it is not meeting the requirements as stipulated. Through CDS, NHG, RCVs can be made more vibrant. The ultimate

goal of CDS is to be self-reliant and to make bastis as beautiful as the city so that they look beautiful and add to the status of the city.

ASSESSMENT IMPACT OF TRAINING

The results are based on questionnaires administered to RCVs. Out of 207 RCV contacted 133 are SC/ST (15%) Reference 1, 98% are female, only 9% of them are above Matric, 89 % are married, Majority of them (42%) are of the age group between 25 and 40. It is good that 94% were aware of the scheme. Main problems of Basti indicated by RCVs is lack of employment opportunity (85%), 68% people face Health problems, 61% people face the problem of lack of good residential accommodation, 62% people face sanitation problems. Urban Development scheme has started between 3-5 years (65.5%) in most of the area. Most of the RCVs have been elected for more than 1 year. (57%) some of them are elected between 1-3 years 30%. Majority of RCV have received training in the year, 2000, 71%. Training contents are liked by most of the RCVs 54%. The scheme was made clear to majority of RCV 92%. Majority of RCV know the importance of health, hygiene cleanliness 95%. During the training of RCVs all contents are covered (95.5%). Most of RCVs feel that they need refresher training (79%) and 34% feel that duration of training should not be more than 2 days. Majority of RCVs Opine that training arrangements were good. Majority of RCVs remember the names of persons who imparted training 93%, all of the RCVs feel that Resource Persons were intelligent and communicative. Majority of the RCV 99.5% feel that preparation for training was good 39% of RCVs feel that impact of training was good. Majority of RCVs have ability to communicate and motivate 98%. All of RCVs have time for the development schemes 99.5%. All of the RCVs have interest in planning and they encourage community participation. Majority of RCVs feel attitude of Municipal Council staff is good. Some of the RCVs feel that attitude of the councillors is good and they visit the head quarter regularly (66%), Co-ordination between different areas is good 97%. Majority of RCVs feel that training lead to confidence building 96%. Most of RCVs get loan easily 58%. Overall impact of urban development is good 48%.

RCVs are the pillars of this scheme as NHG and CDS would be constituted out of them. The success of the scheme depends on their training and implementation of the ideas learnt during the training. The following issues and problems need analysis, which are based on our personnel observation and discussions:

(1) Training which is imparted to RCV is a mere formality as it is impossible to impart training in 4-5 hours. It requires atleast 3-4 days. A personnel observation revealed that it is just a get-together and not training.

(2) Contents covered are very meager and leave many important aspects.

(3) Trainers lack of motivation and feel frustrated because of lack of comprehensibility on the part of RCV.

(4) No Audio-Visual Aids and Role-playing is used which can make the training attractive.

(5) Community Organisers take the exercise of imparting training not seriously.

(6) RCVs are living in Bastis where the environment is not congenial—there are many problems in these Bastis like prostitution, rape, drainage, gambling. How to cope with these problems is a challenging task. RCVs must be equipped to tackle these problems.

(7) Venue of training is not good. It should be in a good hall and not in the open.

(8) As an incentive RCVs may be provided atleast Rs. 20 per day.

(9) Refresher training in the process of lectures every fortnight on a selected topic by Volunteers may be arranged.

(10) RCVs lack motivation, which should be an essential access of training.

(11) A video of best-managed Basti may be made which can be screened during training. The video

should be self explanatory about the role of RCV in the process of development. SUDA can prepare a video of this type.

(12) Public relations department can show some documentaries specially designed for slum dwellers.

(13) RCV should be well equipped in the art of communication which is a basic in inter-personal relations.

(14) UNICEF may create a training institute for training of Community Volunteers using latest training techniques.

(15) Project staff must devote a lot of time in bring up the community so that they learn the art of participation and involvement. Community Volunteers need to encourage even if they make mistakes.

(16) Community Volunteers may be hammered with the idea continuously that they have to depend more on their own resources.

Training connotes that the trainers can influence the performance of the trainees. The influence takes the form of knowledge, attitude and action. The ultimate success of the training depends upon the change in behaviour of the trainees, who in turn can inject efficiency and effectiveness in their services. Action training is aimed at creating a situation in which employees can act optimally. Morton R. Daview rigthly mentions the need of Action Training. To quote him, "Action training is training designed to achieve explicit, pre-determined results, which will enhance attainment of an objective of an enterprise in a recognizable, preferably quantifiable way. Action Training is designed to solve a problem, to effect change, to implement a policy or to arrive at other observable and predictable results.[10]

"We can not direct the wind, But we can adjust, the sails."

Notes and References

1. Mason Haire, *et al.*, Psychological Research on Pay: An Overview in Personnel Administration, New York, Paul Rigors and Charles A. Myers, 1969, p. 491.
2. Y.K. Bhushan, "Personnel Planning", in Readings In Cooperative Management (Ed.) ICA, New Delhi, Jan., 1977, p. 141.
3. NCUI, Report of the National Workshop: Employer-Employees a Relationship in Cooperative Sector, Delhi, Feb., 10-11, 1977, p. 38.
4. GOI, Report of the 3rd Central Pay Commission, New Delhi, Ministry of Finance, 1973, Vol. I, p. 49.
5. GOI, A.R.C. Report of the Study Team on Promotion Policies, It Conduct Rules, Discipline and Morale, Vols. I and II, Delhi, 1967, p. 72.
6. Gabriel V. Legisias, College of Public Administration, University of Philippines, "Administrative Capability as a Neglected Dimension in the Implementation of Development Programmes and Project," Sevently General Assembly and Conference of EROPA on "Implementation of the Problem of Achieving Results", October 24-31, 1973, Vol. III, pp. 3-14.
7. Saul M. Katz, "A Methodological Note on Appraising Administrative Capability for Development" in Appraising Administrative Capability for Development, (UN Publication Sales No. E60, II, H.2), p. 8.
8. *Ibid.*, pp. 99-100.
9. Jawaharlal Nehru and Public Administration, IIPA, New Delhi, 1975, p. 88.
10. Morton R. Daview, Organizing For Training, IJPA, January-March, 1992.

7

Perception, Attitude and Co-operation of Beneficiaries

RELATIONSHIP

Public administration and citizens are intimately related to each other as the existence of one without the other is not possible in a civilized society. The harmonious relationship depends upon the sincerity, earnestness and cooperation between the two. To quote Robson, "The achievement of good relations between the government and the public is a matter which does not by any means depend solely on the conduct of civil servants and politicians. It depends equally on the attitude of citizens, groups, corporations, associations of all kinds and, indeed, of all unofficial bodies to public authorities. If we want public servants to behave well towards us, we must behave well towards them. Moreover, we must normally assume that they for their part will behave well...if politicians and civil servants are held in low esteem, if their work is derived, if abuse and invective is poured on them continuously, if loose and unsubstantial allegations are made about their incompetence, dishonesty, laziness and indifference tot he public interests, it is unlikely that officials will develop or display qualities of integrity, industry and public spirit."[1]

Benefits

Good citizen's administrative relationship would:

(a) Encourage people's participation-a sine qua non for development and modernization;
(b) Kindle the potential energy of the citizens into kinetic energy to accelerate development;
(c) Supplement the efforts of the Government in the conduct of its affairs;
(d) Strengthen the values of democracy in the minds and spirit of the people;
(e) Enlist respect in the Constitution which is rooted in people's sovereignty;
(f) Develop bonds of friendship and goodwill between citizens and administration, and viceversa; and
(g) Avoid social unrest, tensions, violence and other social upheavals, which have become the order of the day.

Administration is never something apart from people and their needs; rather it is the means by which these needs are met and the administrator who thinks of his organization as something apart from the community will fail to recognize significant problems of the citizens and the administration will not be in a position to deliver the goods.

ARC has also observed in this very connection: "If, in the prosperity of the people, lies the strength of a government, it is in their contentment that lies the security and stability of democracy."[2]

Out of 154 contacted 107 are SC/ST i.e. 69%. Out of all 154 beneficiaries 108 are female (66%). Majorities of beneficiaries have middle level education i.e. 25%. 27% are below middle. Majority of beneficiaries are married 72% only 26% are unmarried. Most of beneficiaries are between 25-40 years of age 63%. Most of beneficiaries are aware of the scheme (99.5%) while (0.5%) are unaware of the scheme. 89% of the respondents feel that there is lack of employment 58% feel that there are less education facilities like anganwadis, creches etc., 59% feel that there is lack of health facilities, 57%

feel there is lack of sanitation, 47% feel there is lack of good residential accommodation, 46% feel there is poor status of women while 35% feel there is lack of enthusiasm for general development. 90% of the respondents feel that they have not been benefited much. 83% of the beneficiaries knew the govt. functionaries working in their area like ANM's, Anganwadi and health workers etc. while 17% feel that they do not know any such functionaries.

97% of the beneficiaries are aware of the RCVs, NHG and CDS while 3% are unknown and unaware of the elected representatives of the community, 79% beneficiaries feel that govt. functionaries of departments impart knowledge of cleanliness and vaccination, 72% feel that they impart family planning awareness 56% feel that functionaries of Govt. impart knowledge of primary health centre, 53% feel that they provide information on supplementary nutrition and potable drinking water and 38% feel that the functionaries provide knowledge of sub-centres of the basti. 81% of the government functionaries impart importance of sending girl children to school, 72% give knowledge of child health and women health, 58% give knowledge of Adult Education. 72% of the govt. functionaries and departments give knowledge of subsidy and loan for individual enterprises and 40% give knowledge of the same for group enterprises. 58% of the beneficiaries say that meeting between RCVs, NHG & CDS is held after every month while 36% say it is held after 1 or 3 months. 49% of the beneficiaries feel that they fully participate in the above meetings; 40% partially agree with them 39% of the beneficiaries feel that these meetings are very helpful, 23% feel that these are less helpful while 3% feel these meetings are not helpful in any way.

85% of the beneficiaries feel that harmonious relationships are developed amongst the members through conduct of these meetings while 11% feel partially consented with them as far as relationships are concerned. 71% of the beneficiaries implement the things learnt in these meetings while 25% partially implement the practicability of the learnt material and 3% do not implement the same.

84% of the beneficiaries participate fully and enjoy activities related to implementation programme in the basti while 4% partially participate and 4% do not participate, 55% of the beneficiary participate and contribute in thrift and credit regularly while 48% do not participate in the same, 86% of the beneficiaries have availed loan and repay regularly while 12% do not 86% of the beneficiaries definitely benefit from this scheme, 40% think they are very well benefited from this scheme, 13% feel they are very well benefited while 4% marginally feel so, 47% beneficiaries feel that the impact of urban development programme has been very good, 44% feel it is good and 12% feel they have been aversely benefited from this scheme.

Based on observation and Discussion we mention here the issue and problems of beneficiary with the participatory urban development based on our personnel discussion with some of these.

1. The poorest among the poor are not attended seriously APOs and COs do not do any documentation of the poorest and in the process, they are ignored. During our discussion at Jalandhar, there was a lady having four daughters, 2 of them handicapped, the husband lying on bed with permanent affliction of spinal cord.
2. APOs and COs visit some families with whom they develop rapport and neglect many families in need of them.
3. APOs and COs failed to develop quality of leadership among RCVs so that they can diffuse their ideas in the community.
4. People feel that Govt. functionaries are not in a mood to help them seriously. They provide more of a lip service and even they mentioned corrupt practice in some institutions like banks.
5. People are made dependent through assurance while the main focus of APO and CO should be on self-reliance.
6. The people mentioned that there is very little co-ordination among various agencies of the Government.
7. There is no place in the Bastis where they can

meet regularly and there is no schedule of the visit of APO and CO.

8. People have not properly understood the rationale and philosophy of the participatory urban development.
9. Municipal office and staff do not take there problems seriously and hence they feel neglected.
10. Inspite of all the limitations, there has been some improvements in cleanliness and other activities.
11. As regards, their relationships with the officials to get loan etc., they mentioned the following problems:
    - (i) Unhelpful attitude on the part of the officials;
    - (ii) Inordinate delay in transacting Government business;
    - (iii) Corruption amongst the officials;
    - (iv) Favouritism and nepotism in dealing with the general public;
    - (v) Lack of machinery for redressal of public grievances at the district level;
    - (vi) Delays caused by faulty procedures;
    - (vii) Delays caused by lack of coordination, both inter-departmental and intra-departmental;
    - (viii) Delays caused by excessive work load on the Government officials;
    - (ix) International delays.

It is high time for the Government to continue this scheme with more vigor and vitality so that the momentum created partially can be built on sound footing. The MOUD, State Government, SUDA should pursue this scheme seriously, honestly and as per stipulation to remove urban poverty which cause many problems to city life.

For democracy to be successful at the national level, the grassroots organizations have to be strong. The local authorities have to respond to the felt needs of the people. The Citizens have to have faith in the efficacy of the administrative system so that the distance between people and the government is reduced. The administration, for good governance has to be accessible. In developing countries, it is the government, which initiates and implements development programmes. It must gain support of the people in the discharge of these programmes, particularly at the cutting-edge. Such support would strengthen democracy as well as a positive response of the community to development programme, which should be the ultimate goal of good governance.

Let us now discuss the techniques of People's Participation:

1. Strengthening Public Relations through Mass Media

The creation of awareness is integral to social and economic development. The possibility for the power of communication to liberate the minds and potential of people to critical awareness is real in every field linked to human development and the generation of public will hinges on effective communication of information and ideas that relate to people's needs, aspirations and capacities for progress in thought and action. In this sense, getting development process started is largely the task of information, education and communication through public relations.

Public relations is the establishment of a climate of understanding. It means interpreting the programme of an organization to the public and vice versa.

According to J.L. Mccany:

> "Public relations in government is the composite of all the primary and secondary contacts between the bureaucracy and the citizens and all the interaction of influences and attitudes established in these contacts."

According to Harwood:

> "Public relations may be defined as those aspects of our personal and corporate behaviour, which have a social rather than private and personal significance."

The purpose of public relations is not only to supply information, but also to encourage an understanding and cooperation between the citizens and the public servants.

The objectives of public relations should be to increase prestige and goodwill and to protect the life of the organization by safeguarding it against unwarranted attacks as well as to remove the genuine complaints and grievances of the people.

2. Understanding Public Needs and Values of the Community

The first important step in public relations is to understand the community. Every community is different and there are differences between each local community is different in the same country in terms of their work culture and living standards, family life, social structure, population structure and attitudes. Besides, values, beliefs and customs, religious practices, etc. differ in different areas. There is a need to understand the need of the people based upon this diversity before launching any field operations. How to learn about the people and the community? Some of the important methods are:

(i) Discussion with People

Discussion can be both formal and informal. Discussion can be held with formal groups of the people. However, informal discussions with people in the markets and common places will throw light as to what concerns people most. In ascertaining the health needs of the people, CAN (Community Needs Assessment) surveys are carried out before introducing facilities in the area. Mahatma Gandhi had to tour the country to understand the problems of the country. Jawarharlal Nehru advised bureaucracy not to retire in their cells after work but to mix with all kinds of people, which would provide them with material that is not in their files.

(ii) Study of Newspapers, Magazines and Other Published Literature

A public relations department needs to study the published material wherein people express their needs and mention their likes and dislikes. This is a rich source of information.

(iii) Complaint and Suggestion Boxes

Most of the departments have put complaint and suggestions boxes. The analysis of complaints and suggestions can help the organization in understanding the needs of the people.

(iv) Surveys

A well designed survey, opinion poll, or census can help us to know the reactions of the people about organizations. Research generally uses such survey to understand the problems.

Thus, the understanding of the people is vital for public relations to be effective. Hiroshi Nakajima, Director-General of the World Health Organization, has rightly stressed the need of understanding the people. To quote him:

> "People are the true measure of the success of policies and programmes. At the same time, people are the determinants of success. Experience teaches us that, whether in the most sophisticated cities or in the most remote villages, when people act with determination and understanding in pursuit of goals they deem essential, they achieve success. Previously insoluble problems are solved and resources are mobilized. Miracles happen."[3]

3. Informing People and the Community

Public relations departments/sections need to make the people aware about the people's benefit programmes they want to undertake for the people's benefit or the benefit of the country/area. This would aim at educating the people about the schemes in operation-their objectives, services, eligibility criteria, agencies and functionaries for the delivery of services. A good public relations exercise would provide the information in a way as to generate community's conviction about the efficacy and usefulness of the services. It would also lead to community's clear understanding of its participation and contribution.

4. Creating Satisfactory Climate

For any public relation campaign to be effective, it is important to create an environment of goodwill based on equity. People must be given their due status and must be taken into confidence based on trust.

5. Advising People

The government may advise the people to act in a way, which may be beneficial to them and to the government/ agency concerned. Public relations through its various channels need to inject the desired changes to generate development, dynamism and modernization. Thus, the advice to be effective should be preceded by extensive planning of the public relations strategies to be followed.

The right to participate in the affairs of the country is meaningless unless the citizens are well informed on all sides of the issues, in respect of which they are called upon to express their views. One-sided information, disinformation, misinformation and non-informa-tion-all equally create an uninformed citizenry, which makes democracy a farce when medium of information is monopolized either by a partisan central authority or by a private individual. This is particularly so in a country like ours where about 48 per cent of the population is illiterate and hardly 6.5 per cent of the population has access to the print media, which is not subject to pre-censorship. When, therefore, the electronic media is controlled by one Central agency or a few private agencies of the rich, there is a need to have a Central agency, as stated earlier, representing all sections of the society. Hence, to have a representative central agency to ensure viewer's right to be informed adequately and truthfully is a part of the right of the viewers under Article 19(1)(a) of the Constitution of India.

6. Creating Independent and Attractive Mass Media

The media of any society are among the most important institutions. Democracy without free media is a contradiction in terms. Mass media should be the watchdog of democracy, and not the poodle of the establishment. The media has a greater responsibility today than they ever had to guide the nation and make every citizen conscious of his fundamental duties enshrined in the Constitution.

Public relations can also be carried out with the help of Press.

Press

Press is a very important channel of Public relations, especially in metropolitan cities where literacy rate is very high. However, it has its limitations because of low literacy in developing countries like India. Besides, the press in developing countries does not co-operate with the Government in creating positive atmosphere, which is ideal for development. Rather, the press generally concentrates on negative aspects of the government resulting in alienuation between the government and the people.

Public relations programmes need to be fair, honest, truthful, impartial, open, authoritative and responsive. They must be conducted in the public interest. It should attempt at lubricating Government and public relationship based on trust and confidence.

As media is both under Government controlled and in private sector, there is all the more need to formulate a comprehensive media policy. There has to be a close coordination with the concerned local body and other institutions responsible for programme implementation. The vast potential of the mass media has to be utilized for making different sections of the society conscious of their constitutional responsibilities and fundamental duties while integrating entertainment with socially relevant and useful message in the entertainment programmes themselves.

7. Personnel Communication

The art of developing common understanding about people is vital to bring about change of attitudes and behaviour.

Sociologists have classified the diffusion process, which leads to a widespread acceptance of the programme into five stages:

1. Awareness (the individual's first introduction to a

new idea or practices);
2. Interest (the stage at which he actually seeks further information and background data);
3. Evaluation (the stage of assessment on theoretical grounds);
4. Trail (a limited phase of experiment), and finally;
5. Acceptance or adoption.

Thus, the impersonal methods are relatively simper and even less time consuming. The radio, TV, newspapers, posters, and pamphlets can also help in improving public relations. Experience with personal and impersonal methods of public relations ahs revealed that if both the methods are used simultancouely, one can obtain better results than simply suing one or the other method. Alastair Metheson, Deputy Director of UNICEF's division, remarks on the basis of his research that "to get people to act in ways that conform to new values almost always requires that mass communications be reinforced by personal influence."[4]

8. Need of Empowering the People Especially the Disadvantaged Sections of the Society

Participation has a goal and objectives, which the community commonly shares. This common sharing makes the members of the community come together to take collective action to achieve the common goals. The goal sets the parameters and defines, in different situations, who the participants are? The roles different participants perform depend upon their capacity and capability like skills, technical knowledge, formal position, education, control over funds, connection with those in power, etc.

The hierarchy makes the powerful participants active and others passive. This affects participation in favour of those have the power who make decisions for others.

The poorer groups, who are generally the most affected of the development process, are the least endowed and least powerful. The poor are automatically excluded from the participation process. Decision-making is the first step in the development process. Therefore, a key objective of participation is to find out ways to include the hitherto neglected groups, who are directly affected by the negative impacts of development, in the decision-making process.

Participation is a process of giving weightage to the poorer groups in the development process so that they may have say and control over decisions, which affect their lives; participation is a process of empowering the poorest. The indicator of genuine participation the extent the poorer groups have power over decision-making and over resource management.

74th CAA has taken a hold step in providing reservations to the weaker sections of the society. As a result, majority representation has been provided to them to undo the socio-economic handicaps thrust on them in the traditionally exploitative society. These weaker sections of the society have also been given an opportunity to get elected to the posts of Adhyakshas and Upadhyakshas. If this provision was not made in the act, the disadvantaged groups would have been reduced to mere numbers, having no great say in the decision-making process. Due to their illiteracy, ignorance and social backwardness, they could not have mustered enough courage to stand up to the cause of their communities. Thus, for the first time the local governments have been transformed into a system of people's governance of themselves. They can also mobilized the prospective beneficiaries to participate in the process of planning as well as execution. They can, therefore, effectively initiate a process of bottoms-up approach to development.

There should not be mere participation but empowerment should be entrusted to poor people. Arvind K. Sharma rigthly mentions:

> "This reappraisal attributed poverty not just to a violently iniquitous distribution of wealth and resources but equally to an oppressive system of governance in which power was unequally distributed. This, it was asserted, prevented the majority from participating in the political processes; and, therefore, this majority has no opportunity to influence the decisions, which affect them. The silent majority remains an object of development, not its agent."[5]

9. Need of Attitudinal Changes among Personnel both Political and Administrative Responsible for Delivery of Services

A democratic reorientation of the attitudes of the officials towards the citizens has become very much necessary for both the prevention of the citizen's complaints and their prompt redress. Local Bodies should pay great attention to the opinions of the people. Reorientation of the attitudes of the officials thinking on several fronts such as in service training, recruitment from a wider social base, special assignments in rural areas and the like. The officials of local bodies of today should not only possess traditional service virtues like efficiency, integrity and loyalty but should also shake off all the feelings of exclusiveness and superiority. There should be a desire to establish contacts with the citizens to understand their problems. Unless the change in the attitudes of civil servants as a whole is brought about, all other measures to deal with the citizen's grievances will be of limited use.

In order to restore the faith of the people in the fairness and capacity of the administration, the Prime Minister had inaugurated a Conference of the Chief Secretaries in November 1996 on "an agenda for an effective and responsive administration." The objective of the conference was to make public service more efficient, clean, accountable and citizen-friendly by evolving a concrete action plan. The adoption and implementation of the proposed action plan would require strong political will and commitment from the Central and State Government.[6]

The select committee, of British Parliament, clearly demarcated parliamentary activities of a Member, which needed to be insulated from influence of outside bodies or corruption. The Committee short-listed seven ideals of Public Life as follows:

Selflessness

Holders of public office should take decisions solely in terms of the public interest. They should not do so in order to gain financial or other material benefits for themselves, their family or their friends.

Integrity

Holders of public office should not place themselves under any financial or other obligation to outside individuals or organization that might influence them in the performance of their official duties.

Objectivity

In carrying out public business, including making public appointments, awarding contracts or recommending individuals for rewards and benefits, holders of public office should make choices on merit.

Accountability

Holders of public office are accountable for their decisions and actions to the public and must submit themselves to whatever scrutiny is appropriate to their office.

Openness

Holders of public office should be as open as possible about all the decisions and actions that they take. They should give reasons for their decisions and restrict information only when the wider public interest clearly demands.

Honesty

Holders of public office have a duty to declare any private interests relating to their public duties and to take steps to resolve any conflicts arising in a way that protects the public interest.

Leadership

Holders of public office should promote and support these principles by leadership and example.

The attitudes of change agents need be:

1. Willingness to consult and involve poor, backward and illiterate people;
2. Acceptance of the fact that illiterate people are not unintelligent;
3. Readiness to understand people's view points,

their problems and need;
4. Ability to bear with hardships work with limited facilities and resources;
5. Readiness to go beyond the fixed programme activities and objectives to take up water, food, education, etc., and proper orientation to extend the role from that of medical and health aspects to concern in social-structural and cultural dimensions of development;
6. Ability to share knowledge and skills with all other workers of the project team, village health workers, community volunteers and community in general domestication of the 'professional' and the 'technical'.
7. Genuine sincerity and commitment to the development of the rural, poor and backward sections of the society thus setting a model.

It is of utmost national importance that the civil servants are honest and upright in the discharge of their public duties, particularly at a time when clouds of political uncertainty and instability are hovering over out national life. It is at this time that the civil servants should serve the nation honestly by giving a sense of continuity. If they fail, the future of the nation may be dark.[7]

Prime Minster, Atal Bihari Vajpayee has rightly stressed:

> "My greatest concern today is in the area of implementation. The National Agenda for governance has clearly spelt out our priorities. In the light of these priorities, a large number of good policies, programmes, and schemes have been worked out of course. We have also inherited a large number of good policies, programmes, and schemes from the previous governments. Where we fumble, however, is in implementation them in a manner that satisfies the people. I have said it before, and I say it again, that I cannot accept delays and slippages in implementation. I cannot, because the people cannot. The people want to

see action, and not just hear words of promise repeated again and again. I want to see the entire administrative machinery, from top to bottom, work with a sense of mission and result-oriented approach. I want to see them work with their hearts and minds fully in the administrative responsibility they hold. I want to see them work faster and work better. I want to see them work with a sense of mission and accountability. In doing so, I want to see them without any fear or favour."[8]

10. Strengthening of NGO's/Voluntary Agencies and Ensuring their Accountability

Voluntary agencies have a long history of active involvement in the promotion of human welfare and well-being. Lord Beveridge called them "a private enterprise for social progress". Voluntary agencies came into existence spontaneously, voluntarily and without any compulsion or control to fulfil the particular needs of some groups of people. These agencies are flexible and possess the virtues of human services with dedication. Voluntary action is the soul of democracy as this medium secures the active involvement of the people from policy-making to implementation. It is the life and blood of democracy.

A voluntary agency may be defined as:

"An organization that is administered by an autonomous board which holds meeting, collects funds for the support, chiefly from private sources, and expends money, whether with or without paid workers, in conducting a programme."

According to Dharma Vira:

"Work of voluntary organizations and citizen participation are two sides of the same coin. Citizens work in organizations but on their depends the quality of the service the organizations render. Voluntary Organizations provide a frame for citizen participation. Without effective citizen participation, the organization would only be empty forums."[9]

It is very difficult to provide all the services to the people through the Government, as it is very costly. The voluntary agency can exploit the unused energies of the people for the development of the country. Energy of the people, if unused, cannot be preserved. This unused energy "like the unused vast water resources flowing down in Himalyas is not only wasted like those rivers, but also, like the river waters that take with them the top solid of the Himalayan region causing permanent losses in social erosion, cause permanent damage to the human spirit and will in a community through dependence and frustration born out of ever-increasing level of object poverty over the generations.[10]

Voluntary agencies can help in the programme implementation, collaboration and co-ordination with other activities. They can contribute to social welfare development in many ways through programme implementation. They can.[11]

(1) Provide assistance to develop and/or strengthen local NGO capabilities and activities with particular attention to local community development groups;
(2) Conduct reviews and an assessment of existing development programmes and assist communities in the exercise of their own role in such reviews. A greater emphasis on evaluative techniques will render all new programmes more accountable to real community needs.
(3) Develop innovative programmes placing primary health care in the context of comprehensive human development;
(4) Ensure that their existing programmes and new initiatives promote full participation by individuals and communities in the planning, implementation and control of these programmes;
(5) Expand their training efforts to respond to the need of primary health care programmes, e.g., training of health workers, supervisors, administrators, planners and various agricultural and development workers. Included would be

training schemes, which build on the skills of traditional healers and mid-wives.

(6) Extend their efforts to develop locally sustainable and appropriate health technologies and use of resources, with particular attention to energy, waster, agriculture, sanitation and medical care.

(7) Contribute to the creation of new and effective methods of health education, which enable both individuals and communities to assume greater responsibility for their own health.

(8) Recognize the essential roles of women in health promotion and in the full range of community development concerns;

(9) Further extend their capacity to work with poor, disadvantaged and remote populations enabling them to break the cycle of deprivation, and in this way contribute to the search for greater social justice.

11. Injecting Administrative Reforms to make Process and Procedure Simpler and Accessible

Increased productivity in the developing countries depends to a great extent on the executive branch, which should pursue efficiency with greater determination. The executive branch can pursue its objectives provided the prevailing administrative system is conducive to socio-economic progress. The design of an administrative system is a basic aid to the achievement of its primary objectives; if the design is unsound, the achievement of objectives is likely to fall short of expectations. The administration can provide the means whereby the most effective use can be made of the knowledge and skills of the personnel engaged in different activities. The benefits of modern science and technology can reach the people only if such services are properly planned and effectively implemented. There are no two different opinions on this issue. All agree that without consistent and persistent efforts to achieve perfection of administration, progress in increasing efficiency/productivity is impossible. A scientific approach and determination are important factors in raising administrative efficiency.

Simplification of the procedures should take place into matters like:

(a) Regard for public comfort and convenience;
(b) Speed in disposal of applications;
(c) Minimum inter-departmental/office references;
(d) Reduction in the number of levels required to examine cases;
(e) Reduction in the number of agencies with which the citizen has to deal with;
(f) Supply of detailed information to the citizen as to how is he to go about to receive a certain benefit or approval from administration.

12. Genuine and Well Equipped Machinery to Handle Citizens Complaints: Need to set up Grievance Section at all Levels

A democratic reorientation of the attitude of the officials towards the citizens has become very much necessary for both the prevention of the citizens complaints and their prompt redress. Administrators should pay great attention to the opinions of the people. Reorientation of the attitude of the official towards the citizens is a very difficult task. It will require assault on several fronts such as service training, recruitment from a wider social base, special assignments in rural areas and the like. The public servant of today should not only be equipped with traditional service virtues like efficiency, integrity and loyalty but should also shake-off all the feelings of exclusiveness and superiority.

13. Transparency

Mr. K.R. Venugopal, retired Secretary to GOI, argued that "Transparency of governance and right to information should be fundamental rights of all people." These are the basic guarantees for human and social development (1995).

A similar critique and plea is evident in an analysis of most evaluation studies of the anti-poverty programmes. One can thus safely argue that official thinking on poverty alleviation and sustainable human development is increasingly veering towards a framework that recognizes the inherent limitations of a centralized, top-down hierarchic approach to poverty alleviation. This approach recognizes the importance of NGOs/CBOs in activating institutions of civil society, mobilizing and organizing the people strengthening the institutions of local governance, ensuring accountability of official structures and schemes, and facilitation the development of expertise for local development. Department of Administrative Reforms and Public Grievances in its Documents, "Action Plan for Effective and Responsive Government," mentions that there is a widespread consensus on the need to assure freedom of information to the public and to amend such laws that stipulate unnecessary restrictions on free access of the public to information. Government decisions need not be clouded in secrecy. Except in the interest of national security.

CONCLUSION

The success of the development tasks depends, to a great extent, upon the harmonious relationships between the citizens and administration. Local Body should not function as machinery but in a humane and purposeful way. The people in Local Body should have a sense of dedication, responsibility, be responsive and alert tot he aspirations of the citizens. Citizens, on the other hand, should also provide meaningful cooperation to Local Bodies. Under such an atmosphere, it would be very easy to implement the developmental tasks, to bring about social change and modernization in the country. The strengthening of democracy in its social and economic aspect has to be attained through the participation on the part of the people. A similar shift is evident in international thinking. The UNDP framework for Copenhagen Implementation (1996) outlines the basic goal as sustainable human development, eradication of poverty, job creation and sustainable livelihood, advancement of women, and environment protection and regeneration. It goes on to argue that Empowerment of people is central to these commitments. A citizen's charter as in UK can be useful. To quote the features of the charter:

1. Standards

Setting, Monitoring and publication of explicit standards for the services that individual user can reasonably expect. Publication of actual performance against these standards;

2. Information and Openness

Full, accurate information, readily available in plain language, about how well they perform and who is in charge.

3. Choice and Consultant

The public sector should provide choice wherever practicable. There should be regular and systematic consultation with those, who use services. User" views about services and their priorities are to be taken into account for final decisions on standards.

4. Courtesy and Helpfulness

Courtesy and helpful service from public servants who will normally wear name badge. Service available equally to all, who are entitled to them and run to suit their convenience.

5. Putting Things Right

If things go wrong, an apology, a full explanation, and a swift and effective remedy to be offered. Well published and easy to use complaint procedures with independent reviews, wherever possible to be introduced and maintained.

6. Value for Money

Efficient and economical delivery of public services within the resources, the nation can afford and independent validation of performance against standards.[12]

Notes and References

1. William A. Robson (Ed.), The Civil Service in Britain and France, Hogarth Press, 1956, p. 13.
2. ARC: Interim Report of the A.R.C. on Problem of Redress of Citizens Grievances, p. 7.

3. Hiroshi Nakjimo, 'Editorial: A Grand Alliance', World Health, May-June, 1982, p. 3.
4. UNICEF, . UNICEF News, "Communication: A Tool for Development" Issue, 84/1975/2, p. 18.
5. Sharma, Arvind K., 'People's Empowerment', IJPA, July-Sept. 1996, p. 236.
6. Ray, C.N., 'Citizen's Charter in India: An Overview,' IJPA, Oct.-Dec., 1998, p. 804.
7. .Dubashi, R.P., Administrative Autonomy, IJPA, Oct.-Dec.,-1998, p. 850.
8. Atal Behari Vajpayee, Indian Administration Today, IJPA, Jan. to March, 1990, p. 4.
9. Dharam Vir, Citizen Participation in Encyclopaedia of Social Work, Vol. I, p. 102.
10. Malhotra, R.C., *op. cit.*, p. 11.
11. World Federation of Public Health Association, *op. cit.*, pp. 45-46.
12. See UK Foregin and Commonwealth Office, "Raising the Standards: Britain's Citizen's Charter and Public Service Reform", London, Citizen's Charter Unit, November 1992, p. 6.

8

Conclusion

There is a need to make use of Human Resources through Human Resource Development.

SIGNIFICANCE OF HUMAN RESOURCE

HRD in brief is transformation of Potential Human Resource into Kinetic Human Resources for optimization of the potential capacity of employees. It has been rightly said in a study of the Capacity of United Nations Development System that "Human rather than capital is the key to development."[1] Development is not a mechanical process. It is a human enterprise and its success will depend ultimately on the skill, quality and motivation of the persons associated with it. As professor Iris Claude has commented:

> "In a very significant sense, the identity of every organization...is lodged in its professional staff. Members, stockholders, or citizens may control the organization but they can not do it, the staff is the organization."[2]

It is therefore, by increasing the efficiency, integrity and the intelligence of its personnel that the organization will give itself the real means for advancing towards growth and productivity. The constant improvement of the efficiency of an employee is as much the responsibility of the employee himself as of the organization.

NATURE AND MEANING

HRD is an effort to develop capabilities and competence among employees as well as to create an organizational environment conducive to the employees' development. A.D. Moddie has observed that "Good organization building has to create around it a bracing atmosphere, a prideful tradition of integrity, excellence and fellowship. Human beings breathe this ethos around them almost unconsciously and these traditions make for that ethos."[3]

We may thus define HRD as a process of the development of employees through training, performance appraisals, potential development exercises, communication policies, job enrichment programmes, etc. and building of an organizational climate which may encourage openness, risk-taking, role clarity, awareness of employee's responsibility, increased communication, improvement of personnel policies, management styles, etc., so that employees may be effective in translating their potential energy into kinetic energy and the organization may be benefited in terms of better image, higher productivity, better utilization of resources, etc. HRD in a way involves total management and for HRD to be effective, we have to introduce changes in management at all levels.

ESSENTIAL OF HRD

(a) An urge and desire on the part of the personnel in the organization to find better methods to work;
(b) Requisite skill, attitudes and ability in the persons engaged in HRD;
(c) Proper report between the HRD team/Department and the key personnel in the organization;
(d) Removal of hurdles and irritants from the organization affecting productivity of the employees;

(e) Involvement of the Personnel of the Organization to get a lot of unwritten information for understanding the dynamics of the organization for developing an HRD Programme;

(f) The need for suggesting the introduction of only such indigenous methods, which can be implemented by the HRD section without much cost and resistance. Besides, the need for technical consideration may also be kept in mind;

(g) Use of EDP to keep continuous track of every employee and use performance appraisal, training, etc. to inject change in the desired direction;

(h) Members of HRD team may possess a pleasant personality, common sense, imagination, enthusiasm, objectivity and the sense of humour required to induce favourable changes. It has been rightly said that it is easier to change the mountains than to change the minds of the people;

(i) The HRD section must make all the employees in the Organization understand the implications of new methods through seminars, lectures, role playing or any other method to thwart the potential fears amongst the employees of the proposed changes;

(j) HRD to be successful needs revolution in the total concept of management and not merely sporadic and piece-meal attempts;

(k) The HRD team/section must possess technical competence in HRD, missionary zeal, the capacity to motivate and communicate with the employees, cultural adaptability, the capacity to organize and manage, the capacity to inspire confidence in employees, and finally patience and dignity.

The above mentioned essentials, when understood and implemented, would help employees to contribute professionally and enthusiastically to the performance of their respective tasks in terms of the objectives, policies and targets of the organization, as well as to promote a spirit of team work among them. In this way, HRD would develop both in theory and practice and this in turn would lead to efficiency and economy in management.

CONCLUSION

T.V. Rao suggests that employees of an Organization can contribute tot he maximum growth of an Organization by taking following action:

(a) to acquire capabilities (knowledge, perspectives, attitudes, values and skills) required to perform various tasks or functions associated with present or future expected roles;

(b) to develop this general enabling capabilities as individual so that they are able to discover and utilize their own or organizational development purposes; and

(c) to develop an organizational culture where superior-subordinate relationships, team work, and collaboration among different sub-units are strong and contribute to the organizational health, dynamism and pride of employees.

HRD approach focuses on the optimum utilization of valuable human resource through tapping their potential energy to vitalize, activate and renew an organization to generate dynamism and development.

ADMINISTRATIVE ETHICS

Ethics is the moving spirit of a welfare state. All the problems emanating today in a family or society or Government are the product of ignoring ethics for selfish motives. Ethical government may appear to be harsh for temporary period, but this is the only alternative for a permanent beneficial government. "One could argue that ethical behaviour should in itself be rewarding. However, there are tangible benefits s well. Business is built on relationship with the suppliers, customers, employees, and other groups. The strength of these relationships is largely a function of the amount of trust the parties have in each other . . . Studies have shown that the firms which maintain ethic standards perform much better than others due to the good relationships they have with their suppliers, customers, employees and general public. Thus, ethics are cornerstone of business success."[4]

We get a moral government by creating those conditions within which a moral government can operate. This is done by making it possible for officials to acquire the necessary traits and by the practice of the same. An exemplary public servant, to be specific, is not simply one who obeys the laws and behaves within the confines of law but is also one who strives for a moral government. Such is the duty of those who wish to be involved in the difficult and complex world of government. This is the essence and basis of a moral state.[5]

Public life is in a desperate state today, with vice-regal regalia dominating it with its fierce ferocity and crushing criminality, sounding the death-knell of ethicality, morality, and value-system. There is dire need to save it. Public men-at whatever station of life they function -must be men for the public; leaders must lead; and, most importantly, politicians must stop 'politiking'. Public opinion-must be built up against acceptance and tolerance of unethical behaviour and action by anybody, howsoever high and mighty he may be. Crisis of confidence-which admittedly is a function of culture-must be restored in public life; otherwise, the ancient civilization that we boast of will be no more; there will remain no public, no life, worth living, without ethics.[6]

We must remember that it is the top men in each department who set the tone of the administration. It is they who set the example for those under them to emulate. When the acts of those at the top become tainted, when their reputation becomes shady, they will not be able to enforce high standards of integrity in those below them. It is, therefore, imperative that men at the top should personality the highest standards of personal integrity, probity and rectitude. As Sir Ivor Jennings observed, the most elementary qualification demanded of a minister is honesty and incorruptibility. It is, in addition, necessary not only that he should possess this qualification but also that he should appear to possess it.[7]

An action is noble because of the ideal which one strives; in itself an action is neither good nor bad. It is the motive in the heart of man that makes an act either good or bad. Once we are careful to choose for ourselves the right type of motive to inspire our activities, the achievement is not only spectacular, but the entire effort becomes rewarding in terms of the feeling of peace and sense of fulfillment that floods the bosom. When we work joyously to gain a great ideal or goal. Our efficiency increases—Chinmaya.

If Administration work with ethics in their heart and soul, we are sure to make India a heaven on this earth where people from other parts of the world would seek spiritual, ethical and moral pleasure.Need of dynamism and complete understanding of the rationale of the scheme by E.Os. of the Municipalities and staff to ensure convergence and full impact—on personal discussion with E.Os. and their staff revealed the following which should be remedied as suggested:

1. Executive Officer

Executive Officer and municipal staff lack perception, attitudes, morale and motivation towards this scheme and think that municipality has no role to play in it. Their attitude towards the scheme is negligible. Even it was found that E.O. and staff never meet the RCVs, which come to attend the meeting. This also has affected convergence which is the vital component of the scheme, we suggest the following;

(a) Need of intensive training to E.O. and his staff—E.O. and his staff should be given intensive training in the philosophy and importance of the scheme.

(b) Need of earmarking time in weekly schedule for this activity—E.O. and his staff should provide time in their weekly schedule for this activity. This should be in the nature of guidance to APO,

CO, RCV etc for ensuring the full co-operation of municipal administration.

(c) List of RCV, NHG & CDS, CO/APO etc. should be exhibited at a suitable place in EOs office to give importance to this activity.

(d) SUDA should provide necessary authority to EO so that the municipality can monitor the scheme. The salaries of APO, CO should be paid from municipal funds, which can be replenished by Suda, MOUD, State Local Govt. authorities.

(e) E.O. should arrange programmes with the co-operation of Health Department, Education/ Animal Husbandry etc. to ensure convergence. It was observed that health department, education department and animal husbandry department have many activities common with the municipal activities relating to poverty alleviation programme but lack of awareness among them caused duplication, wastage etc. The State Government should appoint convergence committee or Deputy Commissioner should make the planning cell created under 73rd and 74th amendment active to ensure convergence.

(f) Most of the staff of municipality was not either aware or concerned about the scheme. They can play an important role if involved in a dignified manner.

(g) All the people in the municipal area should be made aware of the new activities of the municipality. They can be motivated to participate telling them that dirty part of the city can be a source of diseases; crimes etc. in the city as diseases can freely travel.

Refer to Newsitern—Ludhiana-Migrant Labour (12.5.2001).

2. Assistant Project Officer

APO need vision and missionary zeal to activise CO and inject dynamism among beneficiaries.

APO is the kingpin of the scheme as she is to provide

leadership, morale and motivation both to CO and RCV, NHG and CDS. It has been observed that she devoted major time in the municipal office and not in the fields. She thinks that her job is bureaucratic type while she is supposed to be a moving spirit. We suggest the following:

(1) Only ladies who have aptitude and missionary zeal should be appointed for this post.
(2) They should devote 80% of the time in the bastis and only 20% in the office.
(3) She should prepare her schedule as well as the schedule of the CO so that it becomes easy for supervision and convergence.
(4) She should develop personal rapport with EO, Health/Education/Animal Husbandry Deptt. to ensure convergence.
(5) She should motivate the people in bastis as well as other people in the city to make them participate in making city beautiful.
(6) She should arrange camps with RCV, NHG, CDS as well as people (Social service minded) to make them known about the scheme.
(7) APO should keep EO and SUDA regularly informed so that they can provide her with necessary facilities.

3. Community Organizer

COs Need to develop rapport with the RCV, NHG CDS through effective information, education and communication.

COs are the agents of social change. However, we observe that they are not much interested in their work because of the following problems.

(1) Their salary is too low i.e. Rs. 4000 fixed and is not commensurate with their qualification
(2) Their area of operation is too large as they can pay only flying visit to Bastis and have failed to develop good rapport with the RCVs etc.
(3) They devote very little time in the fields
(4) They waste a lot of time in traveling as they are

allocated more than one station

(5) They have no place to sit in bastis but for educating the people

(6) Their posts are temporary in nature, hence, they are always worried about their continuance in the service.

(7) They lack in the art and science of people's participation

(8) They have poor liaison with EO, Municipal Councillors and SUDA

(9) No duty roaster was made. We must attend to all these problems to mark the scheme function.

(10) Training of RCV needs improvment. Need of equipping them with art and science of community development.

4. RCV

(1) Training of RCV should spread over for atleast five days (each day, suitable 3-4 hours on an important area). One day training including inauguration, registration cannot be effective.

(2) The objective of all task should be to create self confidence, motivation and encouragement.

(3) The talks should be in as simple a language as possible.

(4) Training should be repeated frequently as it is very difficult to change. It has been rightly said that 'It is easier to change the mountains than to change the minds of the people.

(5) RCVs were not meeting regularly as NHG and CDS resulting into apathy and indifference.

(6) There was poor rapport between CO and RCVs which need intimate relationship.

(7) Training contents need improvement. These should cover as explained earlier in Chapter.

(8) Trainers were not optimistic about the outcome of training. There is a need to brief the trainers properly about the scheme so that they can impart knowledge which can make a success of

participatory urban development.

(9) Some of the RCVs who show good talent may be identified and used as Resource Persons as the trainees can understand better from their own persons. Besides, they are able to remind and advise them constantly. In this way, we would be able to develop a team of trainers available locally understanding their community and without much cost.

(10) Those RCVs who are educated, and have interest in the programme may be used as opinion headers.

5. NHC

A personnel discussion and observation revealed the following:

(1) NHC is an essential intitution as it is very near to the families. RCVs have to make all the women living in neighbourhood co-operated in the development of Bastis. Since many of the families have difference on various counts, RCVs with the help of Community Organizer should first solve their problems and make the NHC and ultimately NGC harmonious.

(2) NHC members have no faith in some of the RCV who try to get benefit only for them. Community Organizer should remove such doubts and create confidence in them.

(3) Neighbourhood problems can be solved only by NHC and not by outsiders. Therefore, they should be given training in appropriate technology.

(4) Neighbourhood Group, so far, is depending on Government and are not moving forwards self-reliance.

(5) Community Organizers because of lack of time have failed to motivate them to participate.

(6) They lack the aptitude for development, which need be included by COs.

We can thus say that development is a challenging and arduous task, which require the dedication, hard work and sincerity on the part of the Community Organizer. Once the inertia of the members of NHC is removed, they can accelerate the momentum of development.

6. CDS

Based on discussion and observation, we mention here the following issues and problems, which need attention of MOUD, State Government and SUDA.

1. CDS is an apex Organization in the overall process of urban participatory development but one feels sad when it is found that CDS either does not exist in many places or lying defunct or not registered. APOs and COs should give top priority in getting the formation of active CDS because only through this agency, other agencies take NHG, RCV can be made functional. Macro-approach is essential to reach mirco-level.
2. It was mentioned at many places that the funds allocated to CDS are very meager. Funds need be increased so that activities entrusted to them can be carried out successfully.
3. APOs and COs have not been active in providing technical knowledge and appropriate technology to CDS so that they can improve the quality of life in Bastis. The members of CDS are to be given the ideas continuously as they are entrenched in poverty and have lost the ability inherent in them to think about their potentiality.
4. Members of CDS do not attend the meetings regularly. No record of the meeting is kept. The activities mostly remain in paper.
5. One of the important activity of the CDS is planning. They lack the art and science of planning in which they can contribute a lot. Since the scheme is aimed at to make them self-reliant. APOs and Cos should impart them training in planning. They may invite some experts team the

area, may be retired people who want to give voluntary services, to give them the training in planning.

6. CDS is enamused with the idea that it is a Government scheme and Government would provide all facilities to them while the actual fact is that they have to develop themselves with little support of Government as a catalytic agent.
7. CDS has no proper place to conduct meetings. There is a need to provide such a place where posters, literature can be placed. The place can serve as a pivotal point for the exchange of ideas about the development of the area.
8. Members of CDS can form committees so that time can be saved.
9. Executive Officer/Municipal Staff should address the CDS once in a month.
10. Elected members of municipality should develop a given liaison with them, as the purpose of both is the same—to make the city beautiful.
11. The administrative structure and arrangements of CDS is not known to majority of its functionaries from the NHG. It is, therefore, essential to make CDS active and purposeful. Theoretically, it is very sound but in practice, it is not meeting the requirements as stipulated. Through CDS, NHG, RCVs can be made more vibrant. The ultimate goal of CDS is to be self-reliant and to make bastis as beautiful as the city so that they look beautiful and add to the status of the city.

7. State Level Agencies

State Level Agencies have to provide leadership to the scheme as this agency has been specially created for this purpose. Leadership can be provided if the organizations possess: (i) Good understanding about the programme, (ii) Good interpersonal relations, (iii) Removing hurdles through constant monitoring.

Since the programme relate to social change and economic development of bastis, there is a need to have more programme officers at the SUDA who can provide technical and administrative guidance to E.Os, APOs., COs., RCVs., NHCs. and CDSs. etc.

However, State Urban Development Authority, Punjab has been doing a good work Additional Project Director, Technical Director and other staff takes interest to see the scheme a success.

There is nothing wrong in the scheme as it is conceptually sound and every detail for implementation has been worked out. Ministry of Urban Development and UNICEF have taken great pain to improve the city life for those who are in great distress. Poverty in any part of the city can make the life of other people miserable, as poverty anywhere is a danger to prosperity.

However, implementation of the scheme is not done as anticipated because of a number of problems, which need analysis, review and action. These are:

(1) Municipalities should take responsibility for the implementation of the programme in all earnestness and seriousness. These institutions may be provided with necessary authority, equipment and finances.

(2) The area of APO and CO may be reduced to have more time and intimate interaction with the beneficiaries.

(3) Salaries of APO/CO may be paid out of municipal finances.

(4) Training of RCV which is the most important component need be strengthened:

 (i) duration should be increased from 1 day or 3 to 4 days.

 (ii) contents should be revised to include more items which cost less money but are more beneficial like Health, Education, Cleanliness.

 (iii) trainers need briefing so that they can give them best according to requirements.

 (iv) Refresher training may be given again and again.

 (v) Convergence, a basic essential of the scheme,

should be achieved for optimization.

(1) SUDA should provide the leadership through programme officers.

(2) SUDA should ensure through APO that NHG & CDS meet regularly.

Need

What is required is:

(a) Simple organizational structure, which can be easily comprehended by the people of bastis.

(b) Clear functional roles of RCV, NHC, CDS, APO and CO etc.

(c) IEC in each system should be very simple and clear.

(d) Persons associated with challenging task like Poverty Alleviation should possess missionary zeal and spirit of service.

(e) There is a need to promote convergence of resources and services for bringing in synergetic self-sustaining grass-root level of the poor women.

PROGRAMMES AND ACTIVITIES

The major poverty alleviation programmes in urban areas consist of physical and social development programmes as well as directs assistance to employment generation. Earlier urban poverty alleviation programmes have adopted area approach under Environmental Improvement of Urban Slums (EIUS), beneficiary approach under Nehru Rozgar Yojana (NRY) and community approach under Urban Basic Services for the Poor (UBSP). Now an integrated approach is being promoted under Swaran Jayanti Shahari Rozgar Yojana (SJSRY). The community based approaches used under UBSP has been now integrated with SJSRY. Prime Minister's Integrated Urban Poverty Eradication Programmes (PMI-UPEP) has been launched in the year 1995-1996, covering all the 345 urban centers that have population between 50,000 and 100,000 as per 1991 census. National Slum Development Programme (NSDP) was lauched in August 1996 for slum development. The Swaran Jayanti Shahari Rozgar Yojana (SJSRY) plans to provide gainful employment to the urban poor through encouraging the setting up of self-employment ventures or provision of wage employment. All these programmes are sponsored by the Central Government and currently being implemented in the country are as fallows:

APPROACH AND PROGRAMME OF URBAN POVERTY ALLEVIATION IN THE 10TH PLAN

The 74th Amendment is intended to increase the participation of the people and accountability in administration. State Governments should legislate the requisite amendments to the municipal laws, to clearly devolve the tasks of urban poverty alleviation and slums improvement to the ULBs.

A multi-dimensional strategy is called for, which will focus on empowerment of the urban poor. The community structure under the SJSRY should be made the common pattern and the foundation of all programmes for the urban poor and slum dwellers. This would be an effective way to give the poor a forum to talk about their needs and, given the empowerment of the poor when organized, ensure that their demands are then met.

The personal who deal with UPA programmes must appreciate the many forms urban poverty can take. These programmes must also deal with the policy-related causes of urban poverty such as inappropriate framework of urban services, inadequate coverage of education, health, infrastructure and transport, lack of labour rights and unemployment benefits, land and housing regulations which make it unaffordable for the poor to find housing and push them to disaster-prone and unhygienic areas, lack of safety nets and social support systems, etc.. The designated UPA cell in the ULBs should be sensitized to ensure that the needs of the poor are provided for in investment plans and maintenance provisions.

Capacity building is required for developing communication and inter-personal skills among the people responsible for providing for the needs of the urban poor, for improving the level of services and satisfaction of the beneficiaries, and for providing coordinated services from a number of line agencies. The creation of UPA cells has to be followed up by exposing personnel to techniques of convergence and team formation, communication and planning.

The positive aspect of SJSRY is that it contains the two basic requirements of any programme of poverty alleviation namely, community involvement and empowerment, and employment generation. Evaluation studies show that the progress of the scheme has not been remarkable, but that is no reason to give up the scheme itself. What is needed, instead, is to take corrective measures and improve implementation. Some areas of improvement are:

- The wage employment component should be sued only for building assets and infrastructure, relating to the urban poor, and not for general municipal works. The requirements should be selected by beneficiaries themselves and implementation should be from such lists of works identified by the beneficiaries.
- The guidelines need to be simplified and made more concise, removing all ambiguities and contradictions.
- The component of vocational training should be revamped and the quality of training improved.
- Community organizers and project coordinators should be appointed wherever they are not present, and the persons must be qualified in social work. The role of NGOs in projects should be strengthened. The community structures created under the scheme should be fully involved in the activities under the scheme, including selection and implementation of works, thrift-and-credit groups, group economic activities, etc. These community structures should be encouraged to fulfill their role as pressure groups for highlighting issues relating to their upliftment.
- Monitoring of the project at both the Central and

State levels should be strengthened.

Tackling Urban Poverty

1. The amelioration of urban poverty should be accorded the same priority as that given to rural poverty.
2. 400,000 urban youth should be selected from poor households every year and trained in skills for which there is a demand.
3. Self-employment of the urban poor must be encouraged by an appropriate credit-support programme.
4. Production and market support should be given to the self-employment urban poor.
5. City planning should be geared to provide shelter and sites for employment generation programmes. Local Bodies should be supported in their efforts to create special employment facilities, including worksheds for small manufacturers.
6. The shelter programme should be used to provide employment to the urban poor.
7. Wage employment for the urban poor should be provided through a programme for creation of such urban assets as water supply, drainage systems, land development, etc.
8. The public distribution system should be strengthened to meet the consumption requirements.
9. Community development should be the strategy for the improvement of the living conditions of the poor and an Urban Community Agency should be set up at national level.[8]

The National Slum Policy, which has already been subjected wide debate and discussion, should be given a final form, followed up by implementation.

Performance of NSDP

The National Slum Development Programme (NSDP) initiated in the year 1997 as a scheme of Special Central

Assistance, has been providing additional central assistance to State Governments for slum improvement. However, its performance has not been satisfactory mainly because of the delays at the State level in releasing the funds to implementing agencies. The monitoring of the programme at the Central level requires strengthening. To ensure proper utilization, during the Tenth Plan the NSDP funds should be released for specific projects. States should submit annual plans for projects which will upgrade selected slums to get over the slum characteristics. The existing practice of releasing the funds to the states should be modified to this extent.

Night-Shelters for the Homeless

The programme of construction of Night Shelters for those without homes in urban areas requires rejuvenation. The provision of subsidy under the schem has to be adequate to make it feasible for NGOs working in the field of housing for the poor, to take up construction and operation of the shelters. The NGOs will also need assistance in procuring land, though the maintenance of the shelters can be left to the NGOs themselves. Hence there is need to revise the scheme, raising the grants per bed to realistic levels, so as to achieve the objective of providing a sufficient number of night-shelter. Establishment of special night-shelters for shelterless women and children will be a focal area for the Tenth Plan.

VAMBAY: The Scheme for Housing of Slum-Dwellers

The objective of VAMBAY (Valmiki-Ambedkar Awas Yojana), introduced in 2001-2002, is to meet a long standing gap in programmes for slum-dwellers, namely, provision of a shelter or upgrading the existing shelter of people living below the poverty line in urban slums. Twenty per cent of the total allocation under VAMBAY will be provided for sanitation and community toilets will be built for the urban poor and slum dwellers. Each toilet block will be maintained by a group from among the slum dwellers who will make a monthly contribution of about Rs. 20 per family. Provision of water is also included in the scheme.

The programme is intended to be implementing in partnership with State Governments, who will set up the implementation machinery, arrange for land where required, and arrange for the credit component of the housing programme. The upper limit of Central subsidy will be Rs. 30,000 per unit in Delhi and the five mega cities, and Rs. 25,000 per unit other million-plus cities and Rs. 25,000 for all other cities and towns. The upper limit of the cost ceiling specified for the construction of a new house. The entitlement of the states for funds under the scheme will be in proportion to their slum population.

CONCLUSION

To conclude, poverty eradication should be a long-run objective, but, in short-run steps should be taken to reduce the intensity of the problem, which require integrated efforts of people, government and voluntary agencies. The services, which are provided in urban areas, are not accessible and affordable to the poor due to illiteracy, ignorance and high cost of services. These conditions have been generating a sense of frustration among them and also leading to law and order problems in urban areas. Therefore, the policies and programmes should be designed to reduce their frustration and improve their physical, social and economic conditions.[9]

Notes and References

1. UN: A Study of the Capacity of the UN Development System, Vol. I, Geneva, 1969.
2. Inis Claude, Swords into Plowshares, New York, Random House, 1964, p. 174.
3. A.D. Moddie, The Bureaucratic Culture and Modernity, Asia Publishing House, New York, pp. 106-14.
4. Atul Dhingra and M.R.P. Singh, "Ethics is Making all the Difference" in Indian Management, July 2000.
5. O.P. Dwivedi, "Conclusion: A Comparative Analysis of Ethics, Public and Public Service", James S. Bowman and F.A. Elliston (eds.), Ethics, Government and Public Policy, New York, Greenwood Press, 1988, p. 318.
6. Bata K. Dey, "Ethics-Maladies and Remedies", in IJPA, July-Sept. 1995, p. 461.

7. H.R. Khanna, "Ethics In Public Life, Issues and Remedy", in IJPA, July-Sept. 1995, p. 357.
8. Report of National Commission on Urbanization, 1988.
9. Prasad, C., 'Perceptions of Urban Poor on Anti-Poverty Programmes—An Empirical Study', Nagarlok, Vol. XXIII, No. 1, Jan.-March 1991, p. 68.

ANNEXURE I

Rural-Urban Distribution of Population—India and States/ Union Territories: 2001

S. No.	*India/State/ Union territory*	*T/ R/ U*	*Population Persons*	*Males*	*Females*	*Percent urban population*
1	*2*	*3*	*4*	*5*	*6*	*7*
	India	**T**	**1,027,015,247**	**531,277,078**	**495,738,169**	**27.78**
		R	**741,660,293**	**381,141,184**	**360,519,109**	
		U	**285,354,954**	**150,135,984**	**135,219,060**	
State/Union territory*						
1.	Jammu & Kashmir	T	10,069,917	5,300,574	4,769,343	24.88
		R	7,564,608	3,625,846	3,638,762	
		U	2,505,309	1,374,728	1,130,581	
2.	Himachal	T	6,077,248	3,085,256	2,991,992	9.79
		R	5,482,367	2,754,251	2,728,116	
		U	594,881	331,005	263,876	
3.	Punjab	T	24,289,296	12,963,362	11,325,934	33.95
		R	16,043,730	8,500,647	7,543,083	
		U	8,245,566	4,462,715	3,782,851	
4.	Chandigarh*	T	900,914	508,224	392,690	89.78
		R	92,118	56,837	35,281	
		U	808,796	451,387	357,409	
5.	Uttaranchal	T	8,479,562	4,316,401	4,163,161	25.59
		R	6,309,317	3,143,380	3,165,937	
		U	2,170,245	1,173,021	997,224	
6.	Haryana	T	21,082,989	11,327,658	9,755,331	29.00
		R	14,968,850	8,017,622	6,951,228	
		U	6,114,139	3,310,036	2,804,103	
7.	Delhi*	T	13,728,976	7,570,890	6,212,086	93.01
		R	963,215	533,219	429,996	
		U	12,819,761	7,037,971	5,782,090	
8.	Rajasthan	T	56,473,122	29,381,657	27,091,465	23.38
		R	43,267,678	22,394,479	20,873,199	
		U	13,205,444	6,987,178	6,218,266	
9.	Uttar Pradesh	T	166,052,859	87,466,301	78,586,558	20.78
		R	131,540,230	69,096,765	62,443,465	
		U	34,512,629	18,369,536	16,143,093	
10.	Bihar	T	82,878,796	43,153,964	39,724,832	10.47
		R	74,199,596	38,510,686	35,688,910	
		U	8,679,200	4,643,278	4,035,922	

(Contd.)

ANNEXURE I *(Contd.)*

1	*2*	*3*	*4*	*5*	*6*	*7*
11.	Sikkim	T	540,493	288,217	252,276	11.10
		R	480,488	255,386	225,102	
		U	60,005	32,831	27,174	
12.	Arunachal Pradesh	T	1,091,117	573,951	517,166	20.41
		R	868,429	453,560	414,869	
		U	222,688	120,391	102,297	
13.	Nagaland	T	1,988,636	1,041,686	946,950	17.74
		R	1,635,815	846,651	789,164	
		U	352,821	195,035	157,786	
14.	Manipur	T	2,388,634	1,207,338	1,181,296	23.88
		R	1,818,224	923,428	894,796	
		U	570,410	283,910	286,500	
15.	Mizoram	T	891,058	459,783	431,275	49.50
		R	450,018	233,718	216,300	
		U	441,040	226,065	214,975	
16.	Tripura	T	3,191,168	1,636,138	1,555,030	17.02
		R	2,648,074	1,359,288	1,288,786	
		U	543,094	276,850	266,244	
17.	Meghalaya	T	2,306,069	1,167,840	1,138,229	19.63
		R	1,853,457	939,803	224,575	
		U				
18.	Assam	T	26,638,407	13,787,799	12,850,608	12.72
		R	23,248,994	11,983,157	11,265,837	
		U	3,389,413	1,804,642	1,584,771	
19.	West Bengal	T	80,221,171	41,487,694	38,733,477	28.03
		R	57,734,690	29,606,028	28,128,662	
		U	22,486,481	11,881,666	10,604,815	
20.	Jharkhand	T	26,909,428	13,861,277	13,048,151	22.25
		R	20,922,731	10,660,430	10,262,301	
		U	5,986,967	3,200,847	2,785,850	
21.	Orissa	1	36,706,920	18,612,340	18,094,580	14.97
		R	31,210,602	15,711,853	15,498,749	
		U	5,496,318	2,900,487	2,595,831	
22.	Chhatisgarh	T	20,795,956	10,452,426	10,343,530	20.08
		R	16,620,627	8,290,983	8,329,644	
		U	4,175,329	2,161,443	2,013,886	
23.	Madhya Pradesh	T	60,385,118	31,456,873	28,928,245	26.67
		R	44,282,528	22,975,256	21,307,727	
		U	16,102,590	8,481,617	7,620,973	
24.	Gujarat	T	50,596,992	26,344,053	24,252,939	37.35
		R	31,697,615	16,289,423	15,408,192	
		U	18,899,377	10,054,630	8,844,747	
25.	Daman & Diu*	T	158,059	92,478	65,581	36.26
		R	100,740	63,576	37,164	
		U	57,319	28,902	28,417	

ANNEXURE I *(Contd.)*

1	2	3	4	5	6	7
26.	Dadra & Nagar Haveli*	T	220,451	121,731	98,720	22.89
		R	169,995	91,887	78,108	
		U	50,456	29,844	20,612	
27.	Maharashtra	T	96,752,247	50,334,270	46,417,977	42.40
		R	55,732,513	28,443,238	27,289,275	
		U	41,019,734	21,891,032	19,128,702	
28.	Andhra Pradesh	T	75,727,541	38,286,811	37,440,730	27.08
		R	55,223,944	27,852,179	27,371,765	
		U	20,503,597	10,434,632	10,068,965	
29.	Karnataka	T	52,733,958	26,856,343	25,877,615	33.98
		R	34,814,100	17,618,593	17,195,507	
		U	17,919,858	9,237,750	8,682,108	
30.	Goa	T	1,343,998	685,617	658,381	49.77
		R	675,129	339,626	335,503	
		U	668,869	345,991	322,878	
35.	Andaman & Nicobar Islands*	T	356,265	192,985	163,280	32.67
		R	239,858	128,837	111,021	
		U	116,407	64,148	52,259	
31.	Lakshadweep*	T	60,595	31,118	29,477	44.47
		R	33,647	17,196	16,451	
		U	26,948	13,922	13,026	
32.	Kerala	T	31,838,619	15,468,664	16,369,955	25.97
		R	23,571,484	11,450,785	12,120,699	
		U	8,267,135	4,017,879	4,249,256	
33.	Tamil Nadu	T	62,110,839	31,268,654	30,842,185	43.86
		R	34,869,286	17,508,985	17,360,301	
		U	27,241,553	13,759,669	13,481,884	
34.	Pondicherry*	T	973,829	486,705	487,124	66.57
		R	325,596	163,586	162,010	
		U	648,233	323,119	325,114	

Notes:

1. The total, rural and urban population of India includes the estimated total, rural and urban population of entire Kachchh district, Morvi, Mallya-Miyana and Wankaner taluks of Rajkot district, Jodiya taluka of Jamnagar district of Gurarat state and estimated total and rural population of entire Kinnaur district of Himachal Pradesh where population enumeration of census of India, 2001 could not be conducted due to natural calamities.
2. The figures of total, rural and urban population of Himachal Pradesh state have been arrived at after including the estimated total and rural population of entire Kinnaur district where population enumeration of Census of India, 2001 could not be conducted due to natural calamity.
3. The figures of total, rural and urban population of Gujarat state have been arrived at after including the estimated total, rural and urban population of entire Kachchh district, Morvi, Malya-Miyana and Wankaner taluks of Rajkot district, Jodiya taluka of Janmagar district where population enumeration of the census of India, 2001 could not be conducted due to natural calamity.

ANNEXURE 2

Area and Population

Table 3.16—Population of Towns 1901 to 2001

Sl. No.	Town	District	Population							
			2001(P)	1991	1981	1971	1961	1941	1921	1901
0		1	2	3	4	5	6	7	8	9
Class I (1,00,000 and above)										
1.	Ludhiana	Ludhiana	1395053	1042710	607052	401176	244072	111639	51880	48649
2.	Amritsar	Amritsar	1011327	708835	594844	434951	376295	391010	160218	162249
3.	Jalandhar	Jalandhar	709255	509510	408196	296106	222569	110969	59085	54445
4.	Patiala	Patiala	323309	253706	206254	151041	125234	69850	47531	53545
5.	Bathinda	Bhathinda	217389	159042	127363	65318	52253	24833	20154	13185
6.	Pathankot	Gurdaspur	168275	128198	110039	78192	54810	12354	7353	6091
7.	Hoshiarpur	Hoshiarpur	148243	122705	85648	57691	50739	35345	21285	17549
8.	Batala	Gurdaspur	147753	103367	101966	76488	51300	44458	26122	27365
9.	Moga	Moga	134242	110958	80272	61625	47779	23785	14145	6725
10.	Abohar	Firozpur	124303	107163	86334	58925	46863	21222	8916	—
11.	Mohali	Rupnagar	123284	78457	32351	—	—	—	—	—
12.	Malerkotla	Sangrur	106802	88600	65756	48859	39543	29321	24564	21122
13.	Khanna	Ludhiana	103059	71990	53761	34820	24416	7941	—	—
14.	Phagwara	Kapurthala	10211	88316	75961	55012	37929	16194	11395	14108

Class II (50,000-99,999)									
1. Firozpur	Firozpur	95451	78738	61162	51090	47060	41190	29695	23475
2. Barnala	Sangrur	96397	75430	43680	31847	21354	12341	7741	6905
3. Kapurthala	Kapurthala	84361	64567	50300	35482	29334	26067	16242	18519
4. Mukatsar	Mukatsar	83099	66383	50941	39403	30765	20651	10539	6389
5. Rajpura	Patiala	82551	70983	58645	14840	11211	4735	—	—
6. Kotkapura	Faridkot	80741	62430	47550	34116	32921	20584	14063	9519
7. Sangrur	Sangrur	78717	56419	45220	34015	28344	17132	10799	11852
8. Faridkot	Faridkot	73042	58625	42423	27725	26735	20375	12304	10405
9. Mansa	Mansa	72608	55089	43289	31351	22473	11729	—	—
10. Malout	Muktsar	70958	56868	40533	26746	20774	—	—	—
11. Gurdaspur	Gurdaspur	68417	54733	39529	32064	27665	16641	8906	5764
12. Fizilka	Firozpur	67424	58028	43548	36281	32015	28262	13829	8505
13. Nabha	Patiala	61953	54421	45921	34761	30603	22625	14750	18468
14. Gobindgarh	Fatehgarh Sahib	60672	42063	26637	9387	7026	—	—	—
15. Jagraon	Ludhiana	60106	47372	39683	32999	29617	26704	17731	18760
16. Firozpur Cantt.	Firozpur	57418	53094	44678	41571	46327	41312	24656	25866
17. Sunam	Sangrur	56096	53909	36180	28158	21408	14187	8265	10069
18. Tarn Taran	Amritsar	55587	747529	36903	24116	20961	16607	5988	4428
19. Sirhind	Fatehgarh Sahib	50788	30818	30380	18028	9608	5823	4064	5415
Class III (20,000-49,999)									
1. Dhuri	Sangrur	49290	37431	27100	19300	14835	7649	—	—
2. Rupnagar	Rupnagar	48165	37996	25165	16454	14136	10385	7606	8888
3. Samana	Patiala	46509	36556	31282	21162	16133	14912	9568	10209
4. Nagal Township	Rupnagar	45315	32003	25523	21356	34372	—	—	—

(Contd.)

ANNEXURE 2 *(Contd.)*

0	1	2	3	4	5	6	7	8	9
5. Rampura Phul	Bathinda	44661	35530	31890	23406	19700	9515	4943	4964
6. Kharar	Rupnagar	42415	26109	21807	10686	8216	6072	—	—
7. Jalandhar Cantt.	Jalandhar	40521	31520	33356	33724	42461	24134	11923	13280
8. Giddarbaha	Muktsar	36593	29866	26828	18821	17364	6317	—	—
9. Patti	Amritsar	34432	27776	19765	18389	15833	17595	10439	8187
10. Jaitu	Faridkot	33459	28850	26061	19446	17170	11475	7912	—
11. Jalalabad	Firozpur	32934	23108	16639	11032	7723	7134	3833	—
12. Nawan Shehar	Nawan Shehar	31901	29955	26726	17527	14097	10275	5316	5641
13. Zira	Firozpur	31778	2372	19581	9264	8118	5963	4622	4001
14. Nakodar	Jalandhar	31422	28478	26239	1815	14452	10981	9434	9958
15. Ahmedgarh	Sangrur	28007	25560	16874	12499	9074	4368	—	—
16. Maur	Bathinda	27531	25180	18853	13407	10944	—	—	—
17. Kartarpur	Jalandhar	25152	21093	17878	14644	12202	12150	8512	10840
18. Zirakpur	Patiala	25006	—	—	—	—	—	—	—
19. Raikot	Ludhiana	24738	21061	17106	11709	11239	13777	8379	10131
20. Jandiala	Amritsar	23829	19293	16335	14060	11915	11520	7464	7750
21. Budhlada	Mansa	23499	18717	15968	11713	8620	—	—	—
22. Kurali	Rupnagar	23039	17592	12637	9776	6390	—	—	—
23. Talwara	Hoshiarpur	22580	17379	17907	17865	—	—	—	—
24. Qadian	Gurdaspur	22575	20012	13561	12783	10458	—	—	—
25. Phillaur	Jalandhar	22228	20956	17650	11543	11058	9011	4696	6986

26.	Patran	Patiala	22170	14328	7998	—	—	—	—	—
27.	Urmar Tanda	Hoshiarpur	22115	18786	17665	12262	10383	12734	8362	10247
28.	Morinda	Rupnagar	21788	17440	13502	9326	7540	5837	—	—
29.	Sujanpur	Gurdaspur	21743	16090	13561	12783	10458	—	—	—
30.	Bagha Purana	Moga	21617	17287	14289	-	—	—	—	—
32.	Dina Nagar	Gurdaspur	21494	16968	13078	10607	9599	6968	4047	5191
33.	Karoran	Rupnagar	21379	17813	14454	10937	8676	—	—	3589
32.	Mukherian	Hoshiarpur	20351	—	—	—	—	—	—	—
33.	Longowal	Sangrur	20369	16254	12971	11209	9269	6848	—	—
34.	Dasuya	Hoshiarpur	20118	18351	14657	10363	8721	9206	—	404
Class IV (10,000-19,999)										
1.	Raman	Bathinda	19549	17275	14318	11574	9507	—	—	—
2.	Lehragaga	Sangrur	19310	15555	12241	9531	7847	—	—	—
3.	doraha	Ludhiana	18975	9589	7606	5804	4602	—	—	—
4.	Banga	Nawan Shehar	18892	17721	13490	11885	10212	9112	5089	4697
5.	Tapa	Sangrur	18887	14161	11108	8467	6220	—	—	—
6.	Dhariwal	Gurdaspur	18706	14214	12212	9985	9601	7388	—	—
7.	Ajnala	Amritsar	18602	—	—	—	—	—	—	—
8.	Bassi Pathana	Fatehgarh Sahib	18547	18138	16772	14385	13042	14400	11560	13738
9.	Dhanaula	Sangrur	18397	15967	13885	11877	11238	9560	6886	7448
10.	Machiwara	Ludhiana	18363	13554	9621	—	—	—	—	—
11.	Balachaur	Nawan Shekhar	18106	12466	—	—	—	—	—	—
12.	Sanaur	Patiala	17938	16490	13634	11217	9007	8426	6532	8580
13.	Bhawanigarh	Sangrur	17780	13900	9817	6706	5437	—	—	—

(Contd.)

ANNEXURE 2 *(Contd.)*

0	1	2	3	4	5	6	7	8	9
14. Samrala	Ludhiana	17610	14921	10824	7554	5439	—	—	—
15. Sahnewal	Ludhiana	17248	—	—	—	—	—	—	—
16. Bhadaur	Sangrur	16818	14808	13350	10428	9407	7862	5577	7710
17. Jugial	Gurdaspur	16664	—	—	—	—	—	—	—
18. Adampur	Jalandhar	16620	15331	10960	8105	5177	—	—	—
19. Sardulgarh	Mansa	16315	—	—	—	—	—	—	—
20. Fatehgarh Churian	Gurdaspur	15879	11088	9372	7590	6439	—	—	—
21. Dera Bassi	Patiala	15690	9602	7421	5807	4051	5070	3890	4641
22. Sultanpur	Kapurthala	15653	13722	12143	9176	7661	10168	8141	9004
23. Dharamkot	Moga	15399	11981	9328	7728	6443	8360	5960	6731
24. Hussainpur	Kapurthala	15343	—	—	—	—	—	—	—
25. Goraya	Jalandhar	15138	10708	8802	6000	—	—	—	—
26. Garhshankar	Hoshiarpur	15094	11761	9515	6882	5976	6885	—	5803
27. Bhikhi	Mansa	15078	—	—	—	—	—	—	—
28. Banur	Patiala	15005	10014	7453	5459	4308	—	—	5610
29. Moonak	Sangrur	14928	10686	—	—	—	—	—	—
30. Bareta	mansa	14882	11537	9494	8313	7041	—	—	—
31. Mullanpur Dakha	Ludhiana	14607	10138	8115	—	—	—	—	—
32. Talwandi Bhai	Firozpur	14570	10462	9117	6018	4886	—	—	—
33. Gur Har Sahai	Firozpur	14348	10500	7684	4601	4293	2311	—	—
34. Bhogpur	Jalandhar	13893	4896	6882	—	—	—	—	—
35. Anandpur Sahib	Rupnagar	13886	10674	8576	5000	4189	-	—	5028
36. Bhucho Mandi	Bathinda	13183	10006	7820	2945	2277	—	—	—

37.	Dirba	Sangrur	13073	—	—	—	—	—	—	—
38.	Majitha	Amritsar	13006	10713	9394	8225	6973	9004	5664	6403
39.	Kalanaur	Gurdaspur	12915	—	—	—	—	—	—	—
40.	Goniana	Bathinda	12812	10415	8596	6408	8054	—	—	—
41.	Amloh	Fatehgarh Sahib	12686	9854	7098	4848	3582	2184	1543	—
42.	Shahkot	Jalandhar	12631	10246	7018	—	—	—	—	—
43.	Nurmahal	Jalandhar	12630	11149	9676	8135	6905	8324	6845	8706
44.	Rayya	Amritsar	12620	9122	7049	—	—	—	—	—
45.	Makhu	Firozpur	12173	—	—	—	—	—	—	—
46.	Raja Sansi	Amritsar	12131	10008	—	—	—	—	—	—
47.	Rahon	Nawan Shehar	12046	10771	8671	6607	6316	8065	5947	8651
48.	Khem Karan	Amritsar	11938	—	—	—	—	—	—	—
49.	Amritsar Cantt.	Amritsar	11300	3832	11040	3224	7992	—	—	—
50.	Khanauri	Sangrur	10977	—	—	—	—	—	—	—
51.	Bhikiwind	Amritsar	10269	11958	—	—	—	—	—	—
52.	Nehon	Rupnagar	10158	—	—	—	—	—	—	—
53.	Bhuleth	Kapurthala	10079	—	—	—	—	—	—	—
54.	Mahilpur	Hoshiarpur	10019	—	—	—	—	—	—	—
Class V (5,000-9,999)										
1.	Handiaya	Sangrur	9725	—	—	—	—	—	—	—
2.	Bagowal	Kapurthala	9612	—	—	—	—	—	—	—
3.	Cheema	Sangrur	9347	—	—	—	—	—	—	—
4.	Bhankharpur	Patiala	9118	—	—	—	—	—	—	—

(Contd.)

Annexure 2 *(Contd.)*

0	1	2	3	4	5	6	7	8	9
5. Khamano	Fatehgarh Sahib	8876	6506	—	—	—	—	—	—
6. Budha Theh	Amritsar	8730	—	—	—	—	—	—	—
7. Lohian Khas	Jalandhar	8546	—	—	—	—	—	—	—
8. Ghagga	Patiala	8212	—	—	—	—	—	—	—
9. Rurki Kasba	Patiala	8186	—	—	—	—	—	—	—
10. Dhilwan	Kapurthala	7980	—	—	—	—	—	—	—
11. Haryana	Hoshiarpur	8913	6473	5633	5002	4468	6417	5205	6005
12. Jandiala	Jalandhar	7704	—	—	—	—	—	—	—
13. Bariwala	Mukatsar	7545	—	—	—	—	—	—	—
14. Dera Baba Nanak	Gurdaspur	7493	7380	6212	8338	5288	5872	4333	5118
15. Chohal	Hoshiarpur	7433	—	—	—	—	—	—	—
16. Payal	Ludhiana	7267	5852	5224	—	—	—	—	—
17. Alwalpur	Jalandhar	7172	6468	5851	4732	4539	—	—	4423
18. Maloud	Ludhiana	7160	—	—	—	—	—	—	—
19. Akalgarh	Ludhiana	6600	5564	—	—	—	—	—	—
20. Kotfateh	Bathinda	6493	5611	4973	4308	3808	—	—	—
21. Badhni Kalan	Moga	6373	8572	—	—	—	—	—	—
22. Gardhi Wala	Hoshiarpur	6263	5159	4459	3753	3153	—	—	3652
23. Mullanapur Garibdas	Rupnagar	6143	—	—	—	—	—	—	—
24. Bhaba	Rupnagar	5794	—	—	—	—	—	—	—
25. Ramdas	Amritsar	5790	4765	4123	4322	3153	5397	—	—
26. Ghanaur	Patiala	5754	—	—	—	—	—	—	—
27. Sangat	Bathinda	5396	2731	2859	3531	2874	—	—	—
28. Hajipur	Hoshiarpur	5366	—	—	—	—	—	—	—

Class VI (5,000)									
1.	Bhusiana	Bathinda	4775	—	—	—	—	—	—	—
2.	Daulatpur	Gurdaspur	4544	—	—	—	—	—	—	—
3.	Sham Churasi	Hoshiarpur	4221	3711	3062	2468	2470	—	—	—
4.	Sansarpur	Jalandhar	4061	—	—	—	—	—	—	—
5.	Shri Hargobindpur	Gurdaspur	3993	3461	3215	2430	2341	—	—	—
6.	Bheroli Kalan	Gurdaspur	3369	—	—	—	—	—	—	—
7.	shekhpura	Patiala	1932	—	—	—	—	—	—	—

P = Provisional.

Source: Director, Census Operation, Punjab.

OPINION SURVEY

Questionaire Schedule
for
E.O./C.O's/A.P.O.'s
Administered by

1. Name: ....
2. Place: ....
3. Qualifications:
   Above Matric ....[ ]
   Below Matric ....[ ]
   Middle ....[ ]
   Below Middle ....[ ]
   Others ....[ ]
4. Age:
   Less than 25 ....[ ]
   Between 25-40 ....[ ]
   Between 40-60 ....[ ]
   Others ....[ ]
5. Caste:
   SC/ST ....[ ]
   General ....[ ]
6. Sex:
   Male ....[ ]
   Female ....[ ]
7. Marital Status:
   Married ....[ ]
   Unmarried ....[ ]
   Widow ....[ ]
8. Number of Children?
   Male ....[ ]
   Female ....[ ]
   Total ....[ ]
   None ....[ ]

9. What were your perceptions about the scheme before undergoing the training?
   Give ....[ ]
   Not give ....[ ]
   No Knowledge ....[ ]
10. For how long you are associated with Scheme?
    Less than 1 yr ....[ ]
    1-2 yrs ....[ ]
    More than 2 yrs ....[ ]
11. How many training you have undergone under UNICEF programme?
    One ....[ ]
    Two ....[ ]
    More than Two ....[ ]
12. Have you learnt new points/knowledge from training about Thrift and Credit Society?
    Yes ....[ ]
    No ....[ ]
13. Has the training been effective?
    Yes ....[ ]
    No ....[ ]
14. Are you satisfied with the Training?
    Yes ....[ ]
    No ....[ ]
15. Do you feel all aspects of the scheme were covered during training almost?
    Yes ....[ ]
    No ....[ ]
    Partially ....[ ]
16. Were changes brought in by field level training of RCV'S in the Bastis?
    Yes ....[ ]
    No ....[ ]

17. Whether the trainers involved during the training have contributed in their awareness about different activities?

    Yes .... [ ]

    No .... [ ]

18. Give your specific suggestion for providing better training at town/H.Q. level?

    Training should be practical .... [ ]

    Theoretical .... [ ]

    Training should be given at short intervals repeatedly .... [ ]

19. Were you treated well during the training and your queries/Question were duly attended to?

    Yes .... [ ]

    No .... [ ]

PART B

1. Do you think that RCV, NHG, NHC'S & CDS can promote the quality of life of the poor People?

   Yes .... [ ]

   No .... [ ]

2. Do you think that this scheme has encouraged people's participation in their own development?

   Yes .... [ ]

   No .... [ ]

3. What role do your play in making the success of this scheme?

   Active .... [ ]

   Little .... [ ]

   No .... [ ]

4. Are your satisfied with your jobs?

   Yes .... [ ]

   No .... [ ]

5. What more facilities your need to make the programme a success?

More Money ....[ ]
More Powers ....[ ]
Satisfied ....[ ]

6. Is there a wide scope of work in this scheme if sufficient staff is provided?

Yes ....[ ]
No ....[ ]

7. What are its limitations?

Shortage of funds? ....[ ]
Feeling of groupism ....[ ]
Complex Procedure ....[ ]
Take more time. ....[ ]

8. What is your liasion with officials of municipal committee?

Good ....[ ]
Not Good ....[ ]
Neutral ....[ ]

9. What is your liason with officials of elected representatives?

Good ....[ ]
Not Good ....[ ]
Neutral ....[ ]

10. What changes would your suggest to make a success of the scheme?

Funds made available in time ....[ ]
Subsidy available in time ....[ ]
More Funds ....[ ]
More Control ....[ ]

11. Can you narrate some positive and negative case studies?

Yes ....[ ]
No ....[ ]

If yes give one each.

12. Do you think that such training has helped in poverty alleviation?

    Yes .... [ ]

    No .... [ ]

13. Do you find difficulty in carrying out this work with your normal duty?

    Yes .... [ ]

    No .... [ ]

14. What do you think are the main problems of your Basti?

    (1) Lack of good residential accommodation .... [ ]

    (2) Lack of interest among the people .... [ ]

    (3) Poor status of women .... [ ]

    (4) Lack of employment opportunities .... [ ]

    (5) Lack of Educational facilities .... [ ]

    (6) Lack of Health facilities .... [ ]

    (7) Lack of Sanitation .... [ ]

15. Was the training imparted helped you in carrying out your new role positively?

    Yes .... [ ]

    No .... [ ]

    Partially .... [ ]

16. What has been the change in the status of your Basti since the inception of the schemes related to Urban Development (Tick which is yes).

    1. Better Sanitation .... [ ]
    2. Better Health Facilities .... [ ]
    3. Better Education Facilities .... [ ]
    4. Regular meetings of NHC .... [ ]
    5. Regular meetings of NHG .... [ ]
    6. Regular meetings of CDS .... [ ]
    7. Good relationship with Municipal Staff .... [ ]
    8. Good relationship with Municipal Councillors .... [ ]
    9. Good relationship with SUDA .... [ ]

10. Setting-up Individual Enterprises .... [ ]
11. Setting-up Group Enterprises .... [ ]
12. Easy availability loans from banks .... [ ]
13. Prompt release of subsidy .... [ ]
14. Better relationship among the members of the Basti .... [ ]
15. Better Roads .... [ ]
16. Better Drainage .... [ ]
17. Better Lighting .... [ ]
18. Better drinking Water .... [ ]
19. Better Sewerage facilities .... [ ]
20. Better relationships with other Government functionaries .... [ ]

17. What has been the overall impact of the Urban Development Programmes?

Very Good .... [ ]

Good .... [ ]

Average .... [ ]

Poor .... [ ]

Very Poor .... [ ]

18. Any others suggestions for improvement?

Chapter - XV

OPINION SURVEY

Questionairre Schedule for Resident Community Volunteers (RCVs) Administered by

1. Name: ....
2. Place: ....
3. Qualifications:

Above Matric .... [ ]

Matric .... [ ]

Middle ....[ ]
Below Middle ....[ ]
Illiterate ....[ ]

4. Age:
Less than 25 ....[ ]
Between 25-40 ....[ ]
Between 40-60 ....[ ]
Above 60 ....[ ]

5. Caste:
SC/ST ....[ ]
General ....[ ]

6. Sex:
Male ....[ ]
Female ....[ ]

7. Marital Status:
Married ....[ ]
Unmarried ....[ ]
Widow ....[ ]

8. Number of Children?
Male ....[ ]
Female ....[ ]
Total ....[ ]
None ....[ ]

9. Period of the start of the urban development Scheme?
Less than 3 yrs ....[ ]
Between 3-5 yrs ....[ ]
More than 5 yrs ....[ ]

10. Are you aware of the schemes started by Govt. through local self govt. to improve the life of the people in your area?
Yes ....[ ]
No ....[ ]

11. When were you elected as RCV ?
    Less than 1 yr ....[ ]
    More than 1 yr..[ ]
12. For how long have you been functioning as RCV?
    Less than 1 Year ....[ ]
    Between 1-3 Years ....[ ]
    More than 3 Years...[ ]
13. When did you get the Training?
    This year, 2000 ....[ ]
    Last year, 1999..[ ]
    No ....[ ]
14. Are you satisfied with the contents of the Training?
    Very Satisfied ....[ ]
    Good ....[ ]
    Average ....[ ]
    Poor..[ ]
    Unsatisfied...[ ]
15. Has the scheme been made clear to you during the Training?
    Yes..[ ]
    No ....[ ]
16. Do you understand clearly the importance of education?
    Yes..[ ]
    No ....[ ]
17. Do you understand clearly the importance of health?
    Yes..[ ]
    No ....[ ]
18. Do you understand clearly the importance of hygiene?
    Yes..[ ]
    No ....[ ]

19. Do you understand clearly the importance of cleanliness?

Yes .... [ ]

No .... [ ]

20. Do you think it has increased your confidence and ability?

Yes .... [ ]

No .... [ ]

21. Do you think that the topics covered were sufficient?

Yes .... [ ]

No .... [ ]

If not, what more would you suggest for the Training?

22. Do you require refresher training to revise & up date the contents already taught?

Yes .... [ ]

No .... [ ]

23. Do you think one day Training Programme was sufficient?

Yes .... [ ]

No .... [ ]

If not, do you recommend it for more duration?

2 days .... [ ]

3 days .... [ ]

more than 3 days .... [ ]

24. Do you think that place & the arrangements for sitting/training was good?

Yes .... [ ]

No .... [ ]

25. Do you remember the names of the persons who imparted Training to you? ....

Yes .... [ ]

No .... [ ]

26. Were they good in their subject?

Yes .... [ ]

No .... [ ]

27. Were they good in communication?

Yes .... [ ]

No .... [ ]

28. Were they well prepared for the Training imparted to you.

Yes .... [ ]

No .... [ ]

Impact

29. What is your impression about the overall impact of Training?

Very Good .... [ ]

Good .... [ ]

Satisfactory Poor .... [ ]

Very Poor .... [ ]

30. Do you feel that you can communicate better with the Community after this Training?

Yes .... [ ]

No .... [ ]

31. Can you motivate the people to lead better quality of life through their own efforts?

Yes .... [ ]

No .... [ ]

32. Do you think that you can serve as a channel of information & communication among the families in your area about various programmes of poverty alleviation?

Yes .... [ ]

No .... [ ]

33. Do you find time & opportunity to present the views of the group to the council/corporation?

Yes .... [ ]

No .... [ ]

34. Do you take interest in Planning, implementation & monitoring at the neighbourhood level?

Yes .... [ ]

No .... [ ]

35. Do you foster and encourage community participation and community involvement?

Yes .... [ ]

No .... [ ]

36. Do you encourage the community in mobilising their resource for their own welfare?

Yes .... [ ]

No .... [ ]

37. Do you think that the Municipal Officer/staff listen to your views carefully and spend some time with you?

Yes .... [ ]

No .... [ ]

38. Do you think that the councillors encourage you or think that you are encroaching on their authority?

Yes .... [ ]

No .... [ ]

39. Do officials from H.Q. frequently visit you to motivate & monitor your activities?

Yes .... [ ]

No .... [ ]

40. Do you think that there is a coordination in the community in the different areas e.g. Health, Education, etc.?

Yes .... [ ]

No .... [ ]

41. Does the training help you to deal with banks with confidence?

Yes ....[ ]

No ....[ ]

42. What do you think are the main problems of your Basti?

(1) Lack of good residential accommodation ....[ ]

(2) Lack of interest among the people ....[ ]

(3) Poor status of women..[ ]

(4) Lack of employment opportunities............................[

(5) Lack of Educational facilities ....[ ]

(6) Lack of Health facilities ....[ ]

(7) Lack of Sanitation ....[ ]

43. Have you been able to get subsidy to your members?

Yes ....[ ]

No ....[ ]

44. Have you also been able to get loans from the banks for your members?

Yes ....[ ]

No ....[ ]

45. What has been the change in the status of your Basti since the inception of the schemes related to Urban Development (Tick which is yes).

1. Better Sanitation ....[ ]
2. Better Health Facilities ....[ ]
3. Better Education Facilities ....[ ]
4. Regular meetings of NHC ....[ ]
5. Regular meetings of NHG ....[ ]
6. Regular meetings of CDS ....[ ]
7. Good relationship with Municipal Staff ....[ ]
8. Good relationship with Municipal Councillors ..[ ]
9. Good relationship with SUDA ....[ ]
10. Setting-up Individual Enterprises ....[ ]

11. Setting-up Group Enterprises .... [ ]
12. Easy availability of loans from banks .... [ ]
13. Prompt release of subsidy .... [ ]
14. Better relationship among the members of the Basti .... [ ]
15. Better Roads .... [ ]
16. Better Drainage .... [ ]
17. Better Lighting .... [ ]
18. Better drinking Water .... [ ]
19. Better Sewerage facilities. .... [ ]
20. Better relationships with other Government functionaries .... [ ]

46. What has been the overall impact of the Urban Development Programmes?

Very Good .... [ ]
Good .... [ ]
Average .... [ ]
Poor .... [ ]
Very Poor .... [ ]

47. Any others suggestions for improvement?

Chapter XVI

OPINION SURVEY

Questionairre Schedule for The Members Neighbourhood Committee Administered by

1. Name: ....
2. Place: ....
3. Qualifications:

Above Matric .... [ ]
Matric .... [ ]
Middle .... [ ]

Below Middle ....[ ]
Illiterate ....[ ]

4. Age:
Less than 25 ....[ ]
Between 25-40 ....[ ]
Between 40-60 ....[ ]
Above 60 ....[ ]

5. Caste:
SC/ST ....[ ]
General ....[ ]

6. Sex:
Male ....[ ]
Female ....[ ]

7. Marital Status:
Married ....[ ]
Unmarried ....[ ]
Widow ....[ ]

8. Period of the start of the Scheme?
Less than 1 yrs ....[ ]
Less than 3 yrs ....[ ]
More than 3 yrs ....[ ]

9. Do you think that you can identify local problem & priorities, which can be put up before Municipal Council for common welfare?
Yes ....[ ]
No ....[ ]

10. Do you understood community needs, which can form the basis of mini plans?
Yes ....[ ]
No ....[ ]

11. Do you support action of Govt. in you area?
Yes ....[ ]
No ....[ ]

12. Do you provide feed back to agencies about the quality of the achievement of the Govt. plans of Municipal govt.?

    Yes .... [ ]

    No .... [ ]

13. Do you help in building common capacity through training with the help of APO/CO/NGO & other Departments?

    Yes .... [ ]

    No .... [ ]

14. Has this training helped in a way in improving the income of the people especially the women?

    Yes .... [ ]

    No .... [ ]

15. Do you help the Municipal Staff in the recovery of loans from the beneficaries?

    Yes .... [ ]

    No .... [ ]

16. Has the M.C. been functioning actively?

    Yes .... [ ]

    No .... [ ]

17. Do you think the members of NHC are regular in attending the meetings?

    Yes .... [ ]

    No .... [ ]

18. Do you think that they take part in the making rational discussions & come out with feasible ideas for determining of the common problems?

    Yes .... [ ]

    No .... [ ]

19. Do you think that the Role of Municipal Council/PO/ Bank Manger/CDPO/APO/CO/Municipal Start, Is good?

    Yes .... [ ]

    No .... [ ]

20. What do you think are the main problems of your Basti.?
    (1) Lack of good residential accommodation ....[ ]
    (2) Lack of interest among the people ....[ ]
    (3) Poor status of women ....[ ]
    (4) Lack of employment opportunities ....[ ]
    (5) Lack of Educational facilities ....[ ]
    (6) Lack of Health facilities ....[ ]
    (7) Lack of Sanitation ....[ ]
21. What has been the change in the status of your Basti since the inception of the schemes related to Urban Development (Tick which is yes).
    1. Better Sanitation ....[ ]
    2. Better Health Facilities ....[ ]
    3. Better Education Facilities ....[ ]
    4. Regular meetings of NHC ....[ ]
    5. Regular meetings of NHG ....[ ]
    6. Regular meetings of CDS ....[ ]
    7. Good relationship with Municipal Staff ....[ ]
    8. Good relationship with Municipal Councillors ..[ ]
    9. Good relationship with SUDA ....[ ]
    10. Setting-up Individual Enterprises ....[ ]
    11. Setting-up Group Enterprises ....[ ]
    12. Easy availability of loans from banks ....[ ]
    13. Prompt release of subsidy ....[ ]
    14. Better relationship among the members of the Basti ....[ ]
    15. Better Roads ....[ ]
    16. Better Drainage ....[ ]
    17. Better Lighting ....[ ]
    18. Better drinking Water ....[ ]
    19. Better Sewerage facilities ....[ ]
    20. Better relationships with other Government functionaries ....[ ]

22. What has been the overall impact of the Urban Development Programmes?
    Very Good .... [ ]
    Good .... [ ]
    Average .... [ ]
    Poor .... [ ]
    Very Poor .... [ ]
23. Any others suggestions for improvement?

Chapter XVII

OPINION SURVEY

Questionaire Schedule For Community Development Structure (Other than RCVs) Administered by

1. Name: ....
2. Place: ....
3. Qualifications:
    Above Matric .... [ ]
    Below Matric .... [ ]
    Middle .... [ ]
    Below Middle .... [ ]
    Others .... [ ]
4. Age: ....
    Less than 25 .... [ ]
    Between 25-40 .... [ ]
    Between 40-60 .... [ ]
    Others .... [ ]
5. Caste:
    SC/ST .... [ ]
    General .... [ ]

6. Sex:
   Male .... [ ]
   Female .... [ ]
7. Marital Status:
   Married .... [ ]
   Unmarried .... [ ]
   Widow .... [ ]
8. Number of Children?
   Male .... [ ]
   Female .... [ ]
   Total .... [ ]
   None .... [ ]
9. Do you represent needs of all the communities , especially women and children?
   Yes .... [ ]
   No .... [ ]
10. Do you reliaise and link-up with agencies and departments to promote action in the community towards fulfilment of their needs?
    Yes .... [ ]
    No .... [ ]
11. Do you identify specific training and arrange for their imparting the same to people?
    Yes .... [ ]
    No .... [ ]
12. Do you facilitate community surveys to be carried out to identify the genuine beneficiaries for economic and shelter benefits?
    Yes .... [ ]
    No .... [ ]
13. Do you prepare community plans and proposals, mobilising resources from the community, town or other sectoral departments?
    Yes .... [ ]
    No .... [ ]

14. Do you extend help to Bank in coordination with UPE Cell, for ensuring repayment of loans by the beneficiaries in time?

    Yes .... [ ]

    No .... [ ]

15. Do you create small community assets in low income areas in consultation with town UPE Cell and Urban Local Body (ULB).

    Yes .... [ ]

    No .... [ ]

16. What do you think are the main problems of your Basti?

    (1) Lack of good residential accommodation .... [ ]

    (2) Lack of interest among the people .... [ ]

    (3) Poor status of women .... [ ]

    (4) Lack of employment opportunities .... [ ]

    (5) Lack of Educational facilities .... [ ]

    (6) Lack of Health facilities .... [ ]

    (7) Lack of Sanitation .... [ ]

17. What has been the change in the status of your Basti since the inception of the schemes related to Urban Development (Tick which is yes).

    1. Better Sanitation .... [ ]
    2. Better Health Facilities .... [ ]
    3. Better Education Facilities .... [ ]
    4. Regular meetings of NHC .... [ ]
    5. Regular meetings of NHG .... [ ]
    6. Regular meetings of CDS .... [ ]
    7. Good relationship with Municipal Staff .... [ ]
    8. Good relationship with Municipal Councillors .. [ ]
    9. Good relationship with SUDA. .... [ ]
    10. Setting-up Individual Enterprises .... [ ]
    11. Setting-up Group Enterprises .... [ ]
    12. Easy availability of loans from banks .... [ ]

13. Prompt release of subsidy .... [ ]
14. Better relationship among the members of the Basti .... [ ]
15. Better Roads .... [ ]
16. Better Drainage .... [ ]
17. Better Lighting .... [ ]
18. Better drinking Water .... [ ]
19. Better Sewerage facilities .... [ ]
20. Better relationships with other Government functionaries .... [ ]

18. What has been the overall impact of the Urban Development Programmes?

Very Good .... [ ]
Good .... [ ]
Average .... [ ]
Poor .... [ ]
Very Poor .... [ ]

19. Any others suggestions for improvement?

Chapter XVIII

OPINION SURVEY

Questionairre Schedule for Beneficiaries in Capacity Building Administered by

1. Name: ....
2. Place: ....
3. Qualifications:

Above Matric .... [ ]
Below Matric .... [ ]
Middle .... [ ]

Below Middle ....[ ]
Others ....[ ]

5. Age:
Less than 25 ....[ ]
Between 25-40 ....[ ]
Between 40-60 ....[ ]
Others ....[ ]

6. Caste:
SC/ST ....[ ]
General ....[ ]

7. Sex:
Male ....[ ]
Female ....[ ]

8. Marital Status:
Married ....[ ]
Widow ....[ ]
Unmarried

9. Number of Children:
Male ....[ ]
Female ....[ ]
Total ....[ ]
None ....[ ]

10. Are you aware of the scheme started to improve the standard of life of the people in your area?
Yes ....[ ]
No ....[ ]

10. What do you think are the main problems of your Basti?
(1) Lack of good residential accommodation ....[ ]
(2) Lack of enthusiasm among the people for general development ....[ ]
(3) Poor status of women ....[ ]
(4) Lack of employment opportunities ....[ ]

(5) Lack of Educational facilities .... [ ]

(6) Lack of Health facilities .... [ ]

(7) Lack of Sanitation .... [ ]

11. Have you taken any benefit from the govt. schemes?

Yes .... [ ]

No .... [ ]

12. Do you know any Govt. functionary working in your area to guide you for better health, education, child care etc. (Health Guide, TBA, Anganwadi worker etc.)

Yes .... [ ]

No .... [ ]

13. Do you know some women under this scheme from your own area who come to guide you (RCV, NHG, CDS)

Yes .... [ ]

No .... [ ]

14. If yes, how are they helping you (Tick which the respondents say yes)

A Health Awarness

Cleanliness .... [ ]

Supplementary Nutrition .... [ ]

Vaccination .... [ ]

B. Knowledge about health facilities

Sub-centre .... [ ]

Primary Health Centre .... [ ]

Potable Drinking Water .... [ ]

Family Planning .... [ ]

Keep Environment clean .... [ ]

C. Education

Adult Education .... [ ]

Education in Cooking nutritious Food .... [ ]

D. Functional Literacy

Sending Children especially Girl child to School[ ]

Education about Food and Nutrition ....[ ]
Child Health ....[ ]
Women Health ....[ ]

E. Subsidies

For Group Enterprises....................[ ]
For Individual Enterprises ....[ ]

F. Loans

Individual Enterprises ....[ ]
Group Enterprises....................[ ]

15. Does RCV, NHG, CDS hold meeting of the members? If yes, how often?

0-1 months ....[ ]
1-3 months ....[ ]
4-6 Months ....[ ]
No ....[ ]

16. Do you take part in the meeting?

Fully....................[ ]
Partially....................[ ]
No ....[ ]

17. Are these meetings helpful?

Very helpful....................[ ]
Partially....................[ ]
No ....[ ]

18. Do you develop harmonious relationships through these meetings or these result in bitterness?

Good ....[ ]
Partially Good ....[ ]
Bitter ....[ ]

19. Do you implement the things learnt in these meetings at home and convince your family members?

Yes....................[ ]
No ....[ ]
Partially ....[ ]

20. Do the EO Anganwady worker visit your Basti and take interest in your problems?
    Yes ....[ ]
    No ....[ ]
    Partially ....[ ]
21. Do the APO Anganwady worker visit your Basti and take interest in your problems?
    Yes ....[ ]
    No ....[ ]
    Partially ....[ ]
22. Do the CO Anganwady worker visit your Basti and take interest in your problems?
    Yes ....[ ]
    No ....[ ]
    Partially ....[ ]
23. Do the ANM Anganwady worker visit your Basti and take interest in your problems?
    Yes ....[ ]
    No ....[ ]
    Partially ....[ ]
24. Do you take part in any activity relating to implementation and monitoring of the programmes in your basti?
    Yes ....[ ]
    No ....[ ]
25. Do you enjoy participation in the activities?
    Yes ....[ ]
    No ....[ ]
    Partially ....[ ]
26. Do you take interest in thrift and Credit Society?
    Yes ....[ ]
    No ....[ ]

27. If yes, do you contribute regularly?
Yes ....[ ]
No ....[ ]

28. Do you get subsidy for your schemes quickly?
Yes ....[ ]
No ....[ ]

29. Are the loans from Banks made easily available?
Yes ....[ ]
No ....[ ]

30. If not, do they ask some money from you as gratification?
Yes ....[ ]
No ....[ ]

31. Are the loans of Banks being returned regularly to the Banks?
Yes ....[ ]
No ....[ ]

32. Do you think the scheme has benefited the area?
Very Well ....[ ]
Well ....[ ]
Marginal ....[ ]
No ....[ ]

33. Would you like the scheme to continue?
Yes ....[ ]
No ....[ ]

34. What has been the change in the status of your Basti since the inception of the schemes related to Urban Development (Tick which is yes).
1. Better Sanitation ....[ ]
2. Better Health Facilities ....[ ]
3. Better Education Facilities ....[ ]
4. Regular meetings of NHC ....[ ]
5. Regular meetings of NHG ....[ ]

6. Regular meetings of CDS ....[ ]
7. Good relationship with Municipal Staff...............[ ]
8. Good relationship with Municipal Councillors ..[ ]
9. Good relationship with SUDA. ....[ ]
10. Setting-up Individual Enterprises ....[ ]
11. Setting-up Group Enterprises ....[ ]
12. Easy availability of loans from banks ....[ ]
13. Prompt release of subsidy ....[ ]
14. Better relationship among the members of the Basti ....[ ]
15. Better Roads ....[ ]
16. Better Drainage ....[ ]
17. Better Lighting ....[ ]
18. Better drinking Water ....[ ]
19. Better Sewerage facilities ....[ ]
20. Better relationships with other Government functionaries ....[ ]

35. What has been the overall impact of Urban Development Programmes?

Very Good ....[ ]
Good ....[ ]
Average ....[ ]
Very Poor ....[ ]
Poor...[ ]

36. Any others suggestions for improvement?

RCVs Training Programme at M.C. Machhiwara

RCVs/Beneficiaries

After getting training on PLA. Community Organisers discussed PLA Techniques with CDS

CDS Practising PLA Techniques

Bibliography

Anas, A. and Kyu Sik Lee (1998): 'Infrastructure Investment and Productivity: A Framework for Policy Study," Infrastructure and Development, Discussion paper, No. 14', The World Bank, Washington, D.C.

Ashish. Balasubramanian, K. (1988) 'City Functions and City Structure', a Ph.D. Thesis (ISEC). Bangalore University.

Aziz, Abdul, (1984) 'Urban Poor and Urban Informed Sector,' New Delhi:

Bahl, R. and J. Linn (1992): Urban Public Finance for Developing Countries, Oxford University Press, New York.

Development Planning Unit, (2002). *Sustainable Urbanisation—Bridging the Green and Brown Agendas*, DPU, London.

Dhaliwal, S.S., 'Municipal Administration,' Deep and Deep, New Delhi, 1999.

'Economic Survey—2002-2003,' Ministry of Finance, Government of India, New Delhi.

'Financing Urban Development in India,' Edited by Sarma, K.S.R.N., and Published by Centre for Urban Studies, Indian Institute of Public Administration, New Delhi, 1986.

Gallion, Arthur B. and Simon Eisner, 'The Urban Pattern: City Planning Design', D. Van Nostrand Co., Inc., Princeton, New Jersey, 1963.

Goel, S.L. and Dhaliwal, S.S., 'Urban Development and Management', Deep and Deep, New Delhi, 2001.

Guidelines for Property Tax Reforms (2002), Ministry of Urban Development, Government of India, New Delhi.

Hadimani, R.N., (1982) 'Some Perspectives on Planning for Urban Development', Nagarlok, XIV (3): 48-56.

Hanumappa, H.G. (1991) 'Urban Poverty', Jaipur: Print Well.

Hanumappa, H.G., (1981) 'Urbanization Trends in India: A Case Study of a Medium Town', Ashish, New Delhi.

HUDCO (1995): Report of the sub-group on Commercialization of urban Infrastructure Projects, Expert Group constituted by the Government of India, New Delhi.

Jha, Gangadhar (2002), Case Laws on Property Tax and Implications for Reforming the Tax Base, paper presented at the National Seminar on Reforming the Property Tax System in India, organized by NIUA at Banaglore (14-15 February 2002).

Jha, Gangadhar (2002), Development of Municipal Bond Market in India, paper presented at the Workshop on Development of Municipal Bond Market in India, organized by NIUA, New Delhi, 31 May 2002.

Journal of Rural Development, NIRD, Hyderabad, Vol. 21 No. 2, 2002.

Kammier, H, (2002). 'Rural-urban linkages and the role of small and medium-sized towns in development: issues, concepts and policies', ESCAP/UN-Habitat workshop on poverty alleviation through rural-urban linkages: the role of small and medium-sized towns

Mehta, D. (1995): "Municipal Bond Market for Urban Infrastructure," FIRE (D) Working Paper No. 2, NIUA, New Delhi.

Mehta, D. and P. Pathak (1996): Urban Infrastructure Finance in India, Country Discussion Paper presented at the Regional Assistance Seminar on Urban Infrastructure Finance, Asian Development Bank, Manila, Philippines, 16-18 April.

Nandy, Raj, 'Developing Small and Medium Towns,' published by Indian Institute of Public Administration, New Delhi, 1985.

Naude, W. and Krugell, W. (2002). 'An inquiry into cities and their role in sub national economic growth in South Africa', Conference on Spatial Inequality in Africa, Centre for the Study of African Economies, University of Oxford.

Neilson, L. (2000). 'Australia's Capital Cities in a 21st Century Global Economy', Centre for Developing Cities,

University of Canberra.

NIUA (1983): The Resources of Urban Local Bodies in India and the Level of Services provided, Report presented to the Eighth Finance Commission.

NIUA (1988): State of India's Urbanization, New Delhi.

NIUA (1994a): Power to the People: The 74th Constitutional Amendment, New Delhi.

NIUA (1994a): Scope and Practice of Privatization of Urban Services in India. Research Study Series Number 59, New Delhi.

Ramachandran, H., (1982) 'Living Conditions in Bangalore: An Analysis of Residents Perception', Bangalore: ISEC Mimeo.

Rao, M.S.A. (1970), 'Urbanization and Social Change', New Delhi: Orient Longmans Limited.

Rao, N. Baskara, (1991) 'Census Criteria for Rural-Urban Classification: A Need for Re-examination', Nagarlok, XXIII (3): 50-60.

Report of the Eleventh Finance Commission (2000), Department of Economic Affairs, Ministry of Finance, Government of India, New Delhi.

Report of the First Punjab Finance Commission (1995), Department of Finance, Government of Punjab.

Report of the Second Punjab Finance Commission (2002), Department of Finance, Government of Punjab.

Samuel, M.J. (1987) 'Housing Needs in Urban Karnataka 2001 A.D.', Nagarlok, XIX (1): 96-107.

Samuel, M.J. (1995) 'Growing Regionalism as a Barrier to Inter-regional Migration: Evidence from Metropolitan Cities in India', Indian Journal of Regional Science. XXVI (1 & 2): 1-10.

Sassen, S. (2000). *Cities in a World Economy,* Thousand Oaks, California: Pine Forge/Sage Press.

Sastry, G.S., (1985) 'Metropolitan Cities Environment: India,' Nagarlok, 17 (3): 1-11.

Smit, W. (1998). 'The rural linkages of urban households in Durban, South Africa', *Environment and Urbanisation,* Vol. 10, No. 1, April 1998.

South African Government, (2001). 'The integrated rural development strategy', second draft.

Sovani, N.V. and V.M. Dandekar (1961). 'Changing India', (Ed.) Bombay: Asia Publishing House.

Srinivas, M.B. (1966), 'Social Change in Modern India', Bombay: Allied Publishers.

Tacoli, C. (1998). 'Rural-urban interactions: a guide to the literature', *Environment and Urbanisation*, Vol. 10, No. 1, April 1998.

The Constitution (Seventy Fourth Amendment) Act, 1992, Ministry of Urban Development, Government of India, New Delhi.

The Punjab Infrastructure (Development and Regulation) Act, 2002.

The Punjab Infrastructure Development Act, 1998.

The Punjab Municipal Corporation Act, 1976.

The World Bank, (2001): World Development Report, 2001, Oxford University Press, New York.

TNUDF (2001), Report on the Activities and Annual Accounts of Tamil Nadu Urban Development Fund for the Financial Year 2000-20001, Department of Housing and Urban Development, Government of Tamil Nadu, Chennai.

UN-Habitat, (2001). *The State of the World's Cities 2001*, UN-Habitat, Nairobi.

UN-Habitat, (2002). 'The Rural Dimension of Sustainable Development', World Urban Forum, HSP/WUF/1/ORG/Paper 1.

Union Budget 2002-2003, Ministry of Finance, Government of India, New Delhi.

Urban Finance (2001), 'Bond Special', Volume 4, Number 1 (March 2001); Quarterly Newsletter of the NIUA, New Delhi.

'Urban Planning and Policies,' Ed. by Yadav, C.S., published by Concept Publishing Company, New Delhi, 1986.

'Urbanisation in Developing Countries,' Ed. by Mohanty, Bidyut, published by Institute of Social Sciences, New Delhi, 1993.

Van den Bos, L. and Helmsing, B. (1998). 'Rural-urban relations and adjustment—a survey of the literature', ISSAS, The Hague.

World Bank (2000). *Cities in Transition: World Bank Urban and Local Government Strategy*. World Bank, Washington.

Index